D1497976

*Your enjoyment of the world is never right
till every morning you awake in Heaven*

THOMAS TRAHERNE

Awake in Heaven

By GERALD VANN, O.P.

"Your enjoyment of the world is never right till every morning you awake in heaven," wrote a great seventeenth-century Englishman. The author of the present book, a distinguished Dominican educator, writer and lecturer, takes these words as the motto for a picture of man, his place in the universe, and his aspirations. He has made his own the comprehensive view of life set forth in the *Summa Theologica*, applying the principles of St. Thomas Aquinas to problems in the world of today.

With that clearness and perception familiar to readers of *The Heart of Man*, Father Vann begins with a brilliant analysis of man's nature. In this analysis are revealed certain presuppositions regarding the existence of God, morality and happiness, belief in Christ and His mission, dogma and freedom, which are discussed in the second part of the book. In the final section he deals with the application of these principles to marriage and education, to art and to politics.

AWAKE IN HEAVEN

by

GERALD VANN. O.P.

LONGMANS, GREEN AND CO.

NEW YORK · TORONTO

1948

LONGMANS, GREEN AND CO., INC.
55 FIFTH AVENUE, NEW YORK 3

LONGMANS, GREEN AND CO.
215 VICTORIA STREET, TORONTO 1

De Licentia Superiorum Ordinis:
Fr. Hilarius Carpenter, O.P.
Prior Provincialis Angliae
die 16a Feb. 1947

Nihil Obstat:
Edgarus Hardwick,
Censor Deputatus

Imprimatur:
✠ Leo,
Episcopus Northantoniensis,
die 21a Mart. 1947

Printed in the United States of America

FOREWORD

This book is for the most part an adaptation of material provided by broadcast talks and other addresses. These were given at different times and on various occasions; nevertheless they do, I think, form a unity, a single argument with some necessary elucidations and applications. The substance of the argument will be found in Part II, which comprises three talks given in the recent B.B.C. series, *What is Man?* But there were a number of points which could only be touched on in the talks, and many things had to be assumed; so that it seemed useful to add the other chapters by way of explication.

The substance of chapters I and XII-XIII was also provided by broadcast talks; chapters V-VIII are adaptations of conferences given at the University Chaplaincy, Oxford; in substance, chapter IX was originally an address given at a *Religion and Life Week* in Rugby, and chapters X and XI make use of papers read to the Plater Dining Club, London, and to the Society for Education in Art at Oxford, respectively. Finally, Appendix B is in substance a paper read to the Aquinas Society, Oxford. The remaining Appendix A is made up from articles previously published in *Blackfriars*. Moreover, in substance, chapter IX was originally published in *Orate Fratres* (U.S.A.); chapter X in the *Irish Rosary*; chapter XI in *Art Notes*; and chapters XII-XIII in *Blackfriars*; the latter chapter also incorporates some material from an article in the *Bulletin* of the Sword of the Spirit. To the editors of these reviews I wish to express my gratitude for their kindness in allowing me to make use of this material for my present purposes.

G. V.

CONTENTS

PART ONE
The Background

If you had gone to Paris in 1256 or so you would have
seen a tall stout man in friar's clothes and doctor's cap,
and the students sitting round on the floor at his feet to
listen to him, and all the university city agog with his new-
fangled notions: Thomas Aquinas, grandnephew of
Barbarossa, the man who had run away from home to be
a friar, and was kidnapped by his family and locked up in
a castle, but had his own way in the end. He was an
extraordinarily humble and gentle person, in spite of his
blood and the power and zest of his mind; but he was
also an entirely fearless thinker: if he thought he had
found the truth he followed it, no matter where it led him.

Somebody once described the entire Middle Ages as
sunk in barbarism and religion. It is doubtful whether
most of us would put it quite like that now. As a matter
of fact, the world Thomas Aquinas was born into was in
some ways very like our own, though in other ways it was
so different. It was different, first of all, because it was
more colourful: you are in an atmosphere of chivalry,
tournaments, troubadours; of the mixture of idealism and
buccaneering we call the crusades; a world in which the
hardships and squalors of everyday life are lit with a
pageantry we have long since lost. You are in Europe's
springtime: the heyday of lyric poetry, the sense of adventure and discovery, the students singing their way across
Europe, and coming of course to Paris. For Paris at this
time is the centre of Europe because it is the centre of

learning, of the life of the mind—and in those days Europe had not yet learnt to judge things simply on their cash returns.

But we should be very wrong if we thought of this as a mentally tranquil period. Far from it. Europe was a unity in the sense that it was Christendom, yes; but its intellectual vigour produced a great intellectual turmoil: and that is why, in spite of all the differences, it was an age very like our own.

In the previous centuries they had been building the structure of society; and it was a task that took them all their time. But the love of learning and culture was not dead; and the twelfth and thirteenth centuries are full of the thrill and zest of renaissance: the renewal of literature, the quest for scientific knowledge, above all, the passionate search for wisdom. But that search for wisdom was made difficult for them, as it is for us, by the din of opposing doctrines. They had just discovered the major works of Aristotle; and those who welcomed them wrangled fiercely about what they meant. But there were many other conflicting schools of thought: there were platonists and neo-platonists, there were Jewish thinkers and Arabs, there were the so-called followers of Augustine, the intellectual die-hards of the day. Some of these people had no belief in God; some had no belief in reason; a good many fell foul of culture and humane learning. Peter Damian said that the devil was the first grammar-teacher because he taught our first parents to decline god in the plural—ye shall be as gods—so that grammar must be of the devil; and a shadier character, Master Konrad Unckebunck, declared that the devil was in the poets. But there were men such as Abelard had been, both theologian and poet; there were men like Thomas's master, Albert the Great, who was both theologian and scientist. The age was unlike our own because of its supreme reverence for the life of the mind; but it was like our own in the fact that there were more problems than there were clear answers to them, and that the problems went to the heart of things. Is there a God? If so, can we know him? If so, what effect will that have on the business and the fun of life—on learning and poetry, on reason and science, on love and laughter, on the politics of the mighty and the economics of everyman?

The clash of opinions was complex and furious; but in the main you can see two opposing camps: the people who held that this life on earth was worth living and had little use for any other, and the people who held that the next life was the only one worth living for and dismissed the present with a shrug. Then Thomas Aquinas pointed out quietly but firmly that both sides were wrong.

What he had to say is of immense importance to us today. We need exactly what he has to offer: a view of the world, and of life, and of all that life includes and means for us, as a single whole.

People sometimes think that he just took from Aristotle what he thought would square with the christian faith, so as to give the faith a sort of rational backing. That is quite untrue. He learned a lot from Aristotle, as he learned a lot from Plato and a host of others. But the whole basis of his thought is this: if it is wrong to give up faith for the sake of reason, it is also wrong to give up reason for the sake of faith. And why? Because in each case you are betraying the truth, In the last resort it is the same betrayal. For truth is one, being God himself.

In its own sphere, then, reason is its own master. All his life Thomas remained faithful to that conviction: he kept reason and faith distinct. But he did not try to keep them apart. On the contrary. What he learned, and taught, was that, if you steer clear of prejudice and superstition, reason can tell you a lot about God and life and the purpose of life. But then you come up against a brick wall: there are mysteries which the mind just cannot grapple with. So you have to learn to be humble enough to listen to what the faith has to say: you examine it rationally and critically, but you must not refuse to listen simply because you did not invent it for yourself—that would be irrational. Then, if you can do that, you find that it dovetails in with what reason had found out for you: it explains and fulfils it; and in the end you find that you have a picture of life as a whole: you have a picture, and a single, coherent picture, of all the things that matter most; and so you have an answer also to the immense problems which reason had to leave unsolved. And you find in particular, not only that reason and faith lead to the same thing, truth, but that religion and life—the life that is love and beauty, work and politics, science and learning— also lead to the same thing, happiness.

That comprehensive view of life as Thomas saw it is set out in the *Summa Theologica*. It is divided into three main parts. In the first part you start with what reason can discover for itself about God; you go on to see how far it can penetrate into the deepest mysteries of the Godhead as revealed by faith—and never perhaps has it pierced more deeply into infinity than here. Then you have the vision of the universe, as a whole, coming from God and ruled by God: the universe as a harmony of graded and interdependent beings, penetrated through and through by the power and presence of God who sustains it. Then there is the study of man in particular, and of his place in the scheme of the universe. Now that scheme of the universe as a whole in its evolution is like a great circular movement, coming forth from God and returning to him; but the scheme is marred by the gigantic force of evil in the world; the circle is twisted awry; and man in particular is not only bereft but unaware of his destiny. So you come to the second main part of the book: the real end of man, and the way to achieve it.

You are in the realm of morals now. You begin with the discussion of the ultimate purpose of life; then there is a deep psychological analysis of the emotions and the role of the mind and will in human freedom; and then you go on to the use we can make of freedom: the actions and habits that restore us to wholeness, to union with God and the universe, so that we begin to live in heaven; or, on the other hand, the actions and habits that harden us in our isolation and our inner lack of harmony, so that eventually we condemn ourselves to complete loneliness and ugliness, and are in hell. And under this ultimate fate that we forge for ourselves for good or ill, and ruled by it, are all the immediate ends of life—so important because it is precisely through them that the ultimate aim is lost or won: there is the sort of life a man chooses, his work, his play, and all the things he loves and does and learns and teaches; there is the social world of economics and industry; there is the world of politics, and the whole vast structure of international order.

But the universe is twisted awry, away from God; the circle is broken; and there is no merely human power that can overcome the power of evil. And so you come to the third part of the *Summa:* to Christ the Saviour, in whose power alone the evil can be vanquished and man and the universe gradually restored—restored through the life and power of Christ abiding with us in his Church and his sacraments, restored to the gladness and the glory which are the infinite fulfilment of the heart's desire.

Now one of the things that make the *Summa* difficult is

its style. At first sight it is very forbidding. It is technical, cold, scientific; it uses an idiom we have lost touch with. Moreover, very often the thought is packed so tight, and expressed so simply and unemotionally, that you do not realize its force and depth and the richness of its implications until someone else makes them clear to you. That is why there is a lot to be said for getting your first view of Thomas's thought from some of his modern disciples who talk our own language: wisdom does not grow old or out of date, but language does. But when you do become familiar with the style there is a real beauty to be found in it. It is impersonal—he was not the Light, he came to give testimony to the Light—but that very fact helps to give it some of its qualities: the joy of the exact word, and the austerity and economy that are so much more satisfying than a good deal of romantic exuberance.

Let us take one very simple example of Thomas's thought and manner from what he has to say about peace —the peace that so many millions of people are longing for, and that we have to work for if we are ever to achieve it at all. If you want peace, real peace, according to Thomas, you have to realize that justice is not enough. Why? What is peace? It is two things. It is first of all concord: and you have concord only when people manage to agree together about something that concerns them all— we might say international trade for example. But peace is more that that. It is also something within the heart of every man. It means that all the desires of the heart are reconciled and unified; for you cannot be at peace if you are all the time being pulled in opposite directions. Now each of these two things—peace within ourselves and peace with one another—can be brought about, according to Thomas, by one thing only: love. Here are his words: Love will bring us peace within ourselves when we love

God with our whole hearts, so that we see all things in relation to him; for then all our desires will be part of one single desire. And love will bring us peace with one another when we love our fellow-men as ourselves, for this makes us want to fulfil their hearts' desire as though it were our own. (We might, in parenthesis, put this in more concrete terms, in terms of the actual needs of the world today. What he is saying in effect is that we have to will, we have to be determined, that all the ordinary men and women in all the countries of the world shall have bread, and work, and freedom to think and talk and worship and make their own lives; and we have to be just as determined that they shall have these things as we are to have them ourselves.) And so, he concludes, we can say that justice produces peace indirectly, because it gets rid of the things that prevent peace; but directly, it is the fruit only of love, . . . for love is the force that unifies, and peace is the unity of desire.

The third part of the *Summa* was never finished. Shortly before he died Thomas said: I can do no more; such things have been shown to me that all I've written seems to me just so much straw. He kept to the end his undaunted faith in reason; but there are ways of coming to know God and reality that go far beyond what faith and reason combined can tell us. He was one of the deepest and boldest thinkers the world has known; but he was also one of the greatest men of prayer. There came a time when he felt he wanted to express the inexpressible, and knew it was impossible. Perhaps that fact in itself is one of the lessons we most need to learn from him, we who sometimes find ourselves thinking that all knowledge of all reality can be confined within the pages of a textbook.

The following chapters certainly lay no claim to be exhaustive. On the contrary, they attempt only to point to a few important threads in the pattern of life—that pattern that Thomas so clearly saw and that we need to see and live again today if our world is not to go down into the darkness. But these pages do not follow the order of the *Summa:* they start from the other end. They attempt to paint a picture of man first of all; then, inasmuch as, in the painting of that picture, certain presuppositions are revealed, these are next discussed; and then thirdly, some of the principles stated are given fuller application to the world of every day—to the things that matter most to us as individuals, and to the things without which society cannot but perish.

The book as a whole then is an answer to the question, What is man? And with that question we begin.

PART TWO

The Statement

Chapter 2: BECOME WHAT YOU ARE

Most of us perhaps have had at some time in our lives the desert island craving: the desire to get away from the worries and responsibilities and entanglements that other people bring on us. And yet most of us if we did find ourselves on a desert island, would not be happy there for very long: human nature is not made like that. Let us try to paint a picture of human nature as in fact it is.

If you paint a group of people in water colours and then soak the paper in water, the colours will run: the outlines of the people will melt into one another; it is as though each person in the group were being drawn into other people's lives, and at the same time were drawing them into his; so that it becomes difficult to say where each one begins and ends. And that does represent one aspect of human life. We are not like cardboard boxes, into which you can put now this now that but which themselves remain the same all the time. When you try to appraise anybody you can see that he is what he is largely because of the way he has shared his life with other people—in love and marriage and friendship, in his work and his social life generally, in politics, in religion.

But again, think of an acorn growing into an oak: that too is a picture of human life. We are unlike cardboard boxes for that reason too: we are always growing, in one way or another. Education is not just a question of putting information into people's heads, as you pack things into a box: it is a question of helping them to use their own powers and interests to grow in the right way and not the wrong way—and to grow on every level of life, in body and mind and emotions and character—till they become indeed like a well-grown oak, strong and straight and able to weather the storms.[1]

But there is a third thing. We say that a human being's life is made up very largely of his contacts with other human beings: but it makes a great deal of difference how he uses those contacts. If, for instance, all his life he lets himself be acted upon, if he remains passive or behaves like a lifeless machine, then he certainly will not grow to fullness of life and he certainly will not be happy. There is something deep in every human being that makes him want to be a maker: and in all his contacts with things and people outside him he is that, or ought to be that.[2] We talk of love-*making*: and we are right: it *is* making something that did not exist before, making the deep union of two people who once were strangers.[3] It is the same with everything else. Home and family are things that we have to make; work is meant to be making—if it is not that it is not human, it is sub-human—and all the things that go to make up social life and political life are forms of making too; and it is all these things together that produce the man and woman who are really alive because they are really makers and therefore responsible fully-fledged human beings.

Really alive; but still perhaps not fully alive. A bird would soon cease to be a bird without the air it lives in and that gives it life. True, if you asked it what element it lived in it would be unable to tell you, it is not conscious of it. And if you asked human beings what element they for their part lived in, perhaps they too would be unable to answer. Or they might say, Oh of course, air—but

[1] Cf. Ch. X.   [2] Cf. Ch. XI.   [3] Cf. Ch. IX.

that is the element the body lives in, not the whole human being. No, St. Paul tells us what it is, or rather who it is, in whom we live and move and have our being: it is God; and the wise men of the world have again and again said the same thing: human beings are meant to be citizens of a greater world than this one that we see with the eyes. All this, yes; but heaven too. We have our being in God as birds have theirs in the air, and fishes in the sea; and if only we make the effort to realize it, if only we try to accept this God-given destiny, then our horizons stretch to infinity. It is not just a human life that we can lead; but in and through those human things there blow the winds of eternity. It is not just to the full stature of humanity that we can grow in body and mind and heart, but to a sharing in the life of divinity. If you look down on a busy city street from a high building and see far below you the little figures scurrying to and fro like ants, you think how tiny, how terribly insignificant: but in each of them there is the spark of greatness, and in some it has been fanned into a great and might flame, an immensity of life and power. They are specks on the earth's surface; but in their hearts there is the infinity of him who is All in all.

That gives us a picture of the whole man: the whole man, not as he is, necessarily, but as he can be and ought to be. And if that is indeed the whole picture then it is easy to see why we are right to hate some of the ways in which men are treated, and right to think that some of the other pictures that are painted of man are false and wrong.

Suppose you paint man as just a machine, an economic machine, with no horizon beyond the factory walls and no freedom, none of the joy of the maker, within the factory? Suppose you paint him as a political machine: his life the routine of the parade ground, his mind and will swallowed up in the service of an impersonal and infallible state, his whole destiny to be the tool of that State? Suppose you paint him as a psychological machine: the prey of his own physical nature, the plaything of forces beneath the surface of his mind, the dark gods that he must adore but cannot see? What are all these pictures doing but robbing man of his birthright? We are *free*. We are free because in fact we are not just machines, not just bodies or instincts. We are free because we have immortal minds and immortal thoughts and immortal longings: and if you ignore these, or try to quell and quench them, you are destroying man as surely as if you blew the earth to bits with atom bombs—as surely and even more horribly.

And what of the ways in which men are actually treated in this world of ours? Why is it wrong, utterly wrong, to govern a nation by means of the concentration camp and the secret police? Why is it wrong to move men and women ruthlessly and violently from their homes, to treat them as cattle? Why again is it wrong to make use of unwilling men and women as subjects for medical experiments? Why is it wrong to make them economic slaves, forced to do work that they hate in order to have bread to live on? Never for a moment think that the only ground we have for condemning these things is some vague feeling of decency or fair play. The reason why these things are wrong is perfectly plain and clear cut and definite, and it goes right down to the roots of human existence. These things are wrong because they are destroying human nature: not just hurting individual human beings, but destroying human nature. When a nation or a race is very degraded, very brutalized, you find that it takes pleasure in destroying beautiful things—lovely buildings, paintings, books, the heirlooms of humanity. But when a nation or a race begins to destroy humanity itself, then you can know that things have come very near to their end.

That is why there could not be a more burning question than this question, What is man? Because unless we can answer that question we may not notice the process of destruction going on: we may not realize that it *is* destruction. Sometimes it breaks out in a particularly vile and dramatic form and then we cannot help seeing and hating it, as we saw and hated the horrors of Belsen. But sometimes it may be going on more gradually and all round us and in a disguised form: and that is terribly dangerous, because we may take it all for granted or welcome it as progress when all the time it is killing the soul of humanity.

What then is man? We have seen the christian answer, the christian picture, in bare outline; and already it gives us a standard by which we can measure the things that are going on in the world, the things that are happening to men and women today. You remember how Christ speaks of the seed growing in the ground: man is meant to be a growing thing. And where does that growth start from? You remember he speaks too of how wrong it is to bury your talents in a napkin: every human being is born with certain powers, abilities; and he has to be taught how to grow to maturity in all those directions we have been thinking of—love, family, work, society—until you can say that the man who possesses them has used them to become fully alive, to become what he is by nature; and then all that growing personality has to be taken beyond the fullness of human life into the fullness of divine life; and then you can say that he is alive indeed.

That is the measure of man's God-given greatness: to know and love the earth and its fullness, and so to be enriched by all the fullness of life of this finite world; to know and love the Infinity of Love that made the earth and its fullness, and so to be enriched by the infinitely greater and fuller life that lies about it and beyond it; and it is by that picture that we must learn to judge the things that are being done to man.

That is the picture; and yet, not the whole picture. There are lives to which this sort of fullness is made impossible: what of them? If all this is God's desire, God's ideal for humanity, why does he so often allow it to be frustrated? If it is through love and friendship and work and social life that men are to worship him and reach up to him, why are so many deprived of these things? If it is his will that man should be fulfilled and happy, why is life so tragic? That is the question we must consider before we can make the picture complete.

Chapter 3: BEYOND TRAGEDY

What *is* tragedy? You think of a life full of promise blighted by death or physical disaster, by terrible suffering in mind and heart, by the frustration of its highest dreams. You think of the love-tragedies of literature; of those terrible stories the old Greeks tell of the crimes of man and the terrible evils they bring in their train, the working out of fate. But these are things that are happening every day; in ways less dramatic no doubt, but perhaps not less terrible. There are the men who know their need and their power to be makers, but who are condemned by political tyranny or economic enslavement to eat out their hearts in mindless drudgery. There are all those who know their need and their power to love and marry and make a family, and who through no fault of theirs are robbed of their birthright. All this is a tragedy: and how does it fit into the picture of man? Why are these sorrows and frustrations allowed? Is it that God cannot prevent them? If so, he must be less than God. Is it that he does not want to prevent them? If so, how can he be the God of love? In any case what becomes of the picture?

First of all, let us make a distinction. There are evils that are made by man and can be fought and remedied by man. Human evil is expressed in cruelty and tyranny and ignorant brutishness and the lust for power; and you see its effects in the social evils with which we are all too familiar. But, as we know too, these things can be opposed and put right if only men have enough intelligence and determination and love of their brother-men.

But there are other evils which cannot be remedied by human means: the tragedies of unrequited love for instance, a woman's inability to bear children when she longs for them, the death of the one person without whom life is a wilderness for us. What are we to say about these?

They take us deep into the heart of the problem of evil. There is evil in the world, that is clear enough; but we cannot understand it unless we realize that it is an immense power, an immense energy, partly human, partly super-human, always working to turn light into darkness, beauty into ugliness, love into hate, and of course it brings upon the world its own inevitable consequences. It brings suffering. And we human beings are a family; and so we are all involved in these consequences, as the members of a family are always involved in the sin and the suffering of any one of its number. It is the whole world that suffers. And what of God? Is he powerless to stop it, or is he callous? No, indeed; so far from callous that he became man precisely in order to share in the suffering and show us how to make something out of it, how to fit it into the picture: the love of God is at the heart of every sorrow, every tear, every cry of pain. And powerless? Again no; but he does not do violence to his creatures, for he is love;

and to some of those creatures, to men, he has given free will, the power to turn against him and to do evil; and he leaves them their freedom, he leaves his love in their hands, precisely because their own love, if it is not a free giving, is not love at all. So Christ does not try to pretend that evil does not exist; he does not tell us to try to escape from it; he tries to show us in his own life how it can be used to *reverse* what sin does in the world: how it can be used to turn darkness into light and ugliness into beauty and hatred into love.

Suppose that fate deals you a heavy blow: what can you do? You can of course give way to blind rage, you can rant and rave and destroy anything that comes to your hand. You can try to drown your sorrows, escape from them, in a whirl of pleasures that stop you thinking. You can give up life altogether, turn your face to the wall, refuse to meet and face reality any further. But if you do any of these things you are giving in to evil; and of course you are surrendering altogether the ideal of life in its fullness, you are throwing away the greatness of your destiny. Christ tells us that there is another way of dealing with tragedy: a hard way no doubt, but a way that, so far from destroying the picture of humanity, perfects it.

You must sometimes have seen in the faces of the old—and not only the old perhaps—a beauty and a peace of a very special kind; and you will have said of people like that, They must have suffered a lot, but somehow through it they have learnt wisdom, they have learnt what love means. And that is the core of the whole thing. They have learnt what love means. Why did God allow sin and therefore suffering? You must see the whole thing, you can only see the whole thing, in terms of love: man turns away from God, he sins and suffers, and then God becomes man and takes on himself the hard and heavy way of the Cross—why? Because now we know in our hearts what we could never have known in a sinless world: we know the *depths* of the riches of love: we know that to say that God is love is not an empty phrase but a tremendous reality—this *is* love, to suffer to the end with your friend—we know what Christ has shown us, that out of suffering we can make our greatest joy and our greatest glory.

Let us take a simple everyday human example. In human love there is an early springtime stage when everything is gay and happy and in harmony, there are no clouds in the sky. And then there comes the second stage: the squabbles and misunderstandings, and perhaps the wrongs that go very deep. But how silly to think that these must necessarily mean the end of everything. Evil remains evil: you cannot justify these things, and they bring suffering in their train. But that is not the whole story. They can become the material of a happiness and a mutual understanding far beyond the range of the early days, because out of them, if they are rightly met, can come new depths of wisdom and sympathy and love, and the patience which is the fruit of love, and the peace which is the fruit of patience. But wisdom, sympathy, patience, peace: these are things that affect the whole of one's life: you are become through them a much richer and fuller personality; and so you can turn to the other aspects of life too, the other forms of making, far better equipped than you were before.

But supposing the suffering is just a negative thing, just frustration: how can life come out of that? There was a man in the nineteenth century called Damien the Leper: a man who went out as a priest to tend the lepers in their colony, and shared with them all the horrors of their primitive hell, and in the end became a leper himself. Think of all the things, the good and legitimate things, he was setting aside in order to do it: but do you think he was less of a man? Or again, think of another simple everyday example: the mother who deprives herself of so many things, so many activities, in order precisely to be a good mother to her children: is she diminished, is she less of a woman? Think finally of Christ himself, who denied himself almost all the things we think of as making life worth living in order to do—not for a few men but for all humanity—what he had come to do: and is there any slightest hint in him of something stunted or withered or weakly, of something lacking to the greatness and fullness of human nature?

No, these things can be, not the frustration of fulfilment, but the way to fulfilment. And whether as in these examples you freely take on yourself these sacrifices, or whether they come to you against your will but you have the strength and the wisdom to make something out of them, the same thing is true. If you can say, I shall make use of this cross, I shall accept this frustration and learn from it, and in the strength of what I have learnt go forth to help humanity in other ways: then you are on the way to fulfilment and happiness and peace.

Tragedy then is not the last word. The christian picture of man does not try to ignore the existence of pain; nor does it treat it as though it were a good thing in itself. Some evil and suffering can be fought and must be fought; and it is part of the very stuff of christianity to fight it because it is part of the very stuff of christianity to love your brother-men. To be a doctor, and heal the bodily pain of humanity: that is a glorious calling. But to fight to remedy the other sorrows that weigh on humanity: that is a glorious calling too, and without it you cannot be fully a man, the picture cannot be complete.

And what of the sorrows, the frustrations, that cannot be fought, cannot be remedied? They too are part of the picture. In our own lives we can make something out of them: we can make them the material of a deeper wisdom and love; and then, when we meet them in the lives of others, we shall be the better equipped to help them; and in that helping, in that sharing or co-suffering which we call sympathy, we shall bring increase both to these others and to ourselves.

Do you remember some words of St. Paul, which tell us that we must go down with Christ into his death that we may rise again with him into his glory? That is not just something to be achieved, as we hope, in some distant future: it is what we ought to be doing every day. Sin produces suffering because sin is selfishness: it is the denial of love, and only love can produce happiness. If we want to be happy, therefore, and to make others happy, we have to destroy selfishness and learn how to love. That is what St. Paul is telling us; and these crosses and frustrations, these are the very things from which we can learn if we will. For every time we accept them and use them for the good of mankind we are denying selfishness and affirming love; and though the denial may be hard as death for us, still we ought not to lose heart or to give way, for the glory follows. The way of love: that is the core of Christ's teaching; and what does it mean but that we can never find the fullness of life by going out selfishly to look for it. He that loseth his life shall find it. If we can learn that life means love, then we shall find life, because we shall be looking for something else: we shall be thinking, not of the life we can have, but of the life we can give; and then all these other things, the things that make us fully man, will have been added to us.

Chapter 4: MAN FULFILLED

Your enjoyment of the world is never right till every morning you awake in heaven: so wrote a great seventeenth century Englishman, Thomas Traherne. Till you can sing and rejoice and delight in God, he goes on, as misers do in gold, and kings in sceptres, you can never enjoy the world.

We have seen that tragedy need never be ultimate: it can be the material of ultimate happiness, because it can be the way God leads his human children to the infinity of love which is their home. Let us try now to see more clearly what that infinity means.

As birds in the air, as fishes in the sea, so is the spirit of man in the infinity of God. We must not think of God as though he were wholly remote from us, we here, he there, as two objects face one another in their separateness. In the infinity of God we live and move and have our being. But we can forget all this, and then it ceases to be a reality for us; and we live, not the fullness of life, but only a sad sort of half-life, active on the surface but underneath lost and silent and dead. Yet it is not easy to know the God who is in us and about us. What must we do?

First, we must try to find God in the depths of our own souls. It means that every day we have to set aside for a short period the ordinary superficial things that keep us busy; we have to learn to be humble and still and adoring; and so little by little we can come to realize the presence within us and about us, and know that this is what matters, that this is the All, the true centre, and meaning, of our lives, and that in the knowledge and love and worship and service of this is our happiness and fulfilment. And in the end, so the men of prayer tell us, if we are faithful, that realization will be always with us, and eternity will have become in truth our home. That is what prayer is meant to do for us.

But there is also the second way. It is the whole world that is thus lapped in infinity; and all the things we see and love in our daily lives, the grass and the trees and the animals, these too are made by God and loved by him and are redolent of his presence. And so we have to train ourselves to realize that too; and then our effort to live in God will be easier, and our joy in the things he has made will be keener and deeper too. You know how your joy in a lovely thing is intensified a hundredfold if it has been given you by someone you love. So it is here. Till you can sing and delight in God you can never enjoy the world. But if you learn to see God's presence in things, and love and praise God for them, then indeed your life is full. St. Francis preached to the birds; but perhaps it would be truer to say that the birds preached to St. Francis. For the power of association is very strong: a thing, a place, associated in your life with someone you love has great power to bring you joy or sadness because always it speaks to you of them; and in the same way, if you learn to associate things with the infinite Love that made them, they will speak to you of it, they will recall it to you, they will bring to your life a richness which all their own beauty in itself could never achieve.

Things are so much what we make of them. For the scientist, the sun is a ball of gas. For the poet, how much greater: an orb of golden fire, a god, the life-bringer. And for the man of prayer, how much greater still, for in it he sees a symbol of the fire of love, and more than a symbol, he sees the actual presence of the Love that made the sun and the other stars.

And so, if only we can find the one thing necessary, the infinity of God, then even this earthly life in itself will be trebly enriched. First, because even though, as St. Paul says, we have nothing, we shall yet possess all things. To enjoy the world we must delight in *God* as misers do in gold: if we delight in the *world* as misers do in gold—selfishly, graspingly, supremely[1]—then we shall never enjoy it, it will bring us not joy but anxiety and worry and fear, and even though we have all the things that money can buy yet we shall possess nothing. But if every morning we can wake in heaven; if we can learn to delight in things because God made them and his presence and love enfold them, then we shall come to love them for what they are in themselves and rejoice in them all, no matter who may have the title deeds; and so the whole world will be ours to enjoy.

Secondly this life is enriched because of the sort of infinity that is then given to the mind. If we can learn to live in company with God, then we shall come gradually to share his mind and the mighty sweep of his knowledge and his wisdom. We shall learn gradually to look on the fleeting moment that mocks us as it passes, we shall learn gradually to look on the march of centuries, the whole tapestry of time, as though from eternity: and that means that gradually we shall learn the wisdom and peace that cast out fear and worry and confusion, we shall learn something of the deep serenity of the sage even in the midst of tragedy and sorrow, for having the eternal as our possession we shall no longer be at the mercy of every wind of fate and fortune.

And then there is the third enrichment: the enrichment of our lives as makers. To make something good and lovely: that is man's creative destiny and it brings him joy. To make something good and lovely for someone we love:

[1]To delight in God as misers do in gold is of course to have their single-minded concentration, not their selfish greed.

that is doubly creative and doubly a thing of joy. But to make something also in and for the love of God, as part of our life with God, that is trebly creative, a threefold joy.

And even if we are robbed of the forms of making we naturally most desire, still we can always be makers, we can always make sympathy and love for our fellow men as part of our love of God; and that is something good and lovely indeed, and a fulfilment of what is greatest in man.

But if we neglect all this that is offered us, then our life must be terribly impoverished. The life that is bounded by the horizons of this world alone is terribly impoverished: how much more so the life that reduces man to a single level of his being, that makes him the slave of an economic system or a political tyranny. And yet the fact remains that we are members of society: and how then can we serve society without losing something at least of this individual greatness and fullness?

We shall find the answer once again in the nature of love. To serve unwillingly, to be forced to serve, and to be forced to serve like a machine: that is indeed an impoverishment. But to serve because love makes us *want* to serve; to serve therefore in a way that is personal, responsible, creative: that is not an impoverishment but an enrichment; for the dedication of ourselves to something other than and greater than ourselves keeps alive in us a side of our nature which otherwise might wither and die: it keeps alive in us the heart of a child.

We know how, in the love of men and women for each other, there is an element, expressed in very different ways yet equally recognizable, the thing that we call tenderness and that finds its purpose and fulfilment in protecting what it loves. A man wants to protect the woman he loves from pain and distress and the hard things of life; but to a woman too the man she loves is always in part a child. And when that childlike quality is lost in a man or a woman then they become hard and repellent, for something very deep in their nature is destroyed. So Christ tells us that unless we become as little children we cannot enter the kingdom of heaven; and we are to pray to God as children to their father, and we are to think of his eternal providence as the tender guidance and protection of the divine arms. And so, to be able to turn all the greatness of humanity to the service of the God we love and the human beings we love and the world we love: that is the way to the final fulfilment of our nature: the Godlike creator who is also always God's creature, the man who is always also the child.

When we look in this way at the greatness of humanity, and then look at the shabbiness, the squalor, the pettiness and meanness, the cruelty and evil of life as in fact it is so often lived, then indeed we might say there is nothing left for us but despair. And yet surely it is precisely the greatness of the picture that must make us hope. There is a power in the spirit of man that nothing can quench; and you can see it most clearly and most magnificently asserted in times of darkness and ignorance and tyranny. Too easily we let ourselves think of power only in terms of material things, of money and machines, of guns and bombs. No, there is the power of man's unconquerable mind and heart; and when a man is fulfilled and shares in eternity, and at the same time keeps alive in himself the heart of a child, then in him there is power indeed; for the might of the Godhead can use him as its instrument, and in the fullness of that power he can stand like a rock and resist death and give life to others, and in and with the Christ who lives in him, can save and heal the world.

PART THREE

The Presuppositions

Chapter 5: DOES GOD EXIST?

It is possible to argue, especially in these days perhaps, that when Aristotle said that man is a reasonable animal he himself was being an unreasonable optimist: there is evidence enough in the world of the irrationality of men. But in fact it is more accurate to retain our faith in reason, as Thomas Aquinas did, and yet to realize that, as the definition of man itself implies, there is always liable to be discord, where sinful man is concerned, between the spirit and the animal. We try to think, and perhaps we think we are thinking, objectively, but in fact the senses and emotions keep running counter to the processes of reasoning. Man is body-spirit, and the two elements often make war on one another, and always affect one another. The mind affects the body: a man can ruin his health by worrying, by misusing his reason; but also the body affects the mind: a man can ruin his reasoning power by sloth or gluttony. And when we realize that it is not only the senses but the emotional life as well that can be in opposition to the reason, then we can see what an army in battle array we may be bringing up against it.

All this may be very relevant if we find ourselves wondering whether God really exists. There is a sceptic in most of us; and sometimes he reveals his presence even in those who normally believe most firmly. And if we do find ourselves faced with this problem, and try to think it out, it is well to make sure first of all that we are indeed reasoning and not, as the psychologists say, rationalizing,

A.H.

not in fact following blindly after our emotional prejudices. For indeed this antagonism between the two levels
of life is most to be expected in the realm of faith and
morals. Sometimes we tell ourselves that we have exa-
mined this or that moral question from every angle and
have failed to find a solution, so that we can only go on as
before: and that is in fact precisely what we wanted to do,
and our emotions have prevented us from seeing the one
cogent reason for changing our behaviour which was
really challenging us.

In this question of God's existence the senses and emotions are meant not to hinder but to help us to God—it is
a point that needs stressing, and we shall return to it later
—but in fact they can do a great deal of hindering: they
can make us blind to what reason, if left to itself, might
well see to be the truth.

To real scepticism we must turn later on; but sometimes the scepticism which reveals itself in us is not
rational at all but emotional. It may be simply a question
of sloth: not wanting to believe in anything at all because
we cannot be bothered. It may be a question of absorbing,
emotionally, a prevailing climate of opinion as wholeheartedly and uncritically as a sponge: of telling ourselves,
for instance, that religion is not scientific: as though any
sane man had ever said that it was; or that what is wanted
is attention to the needs of this world, as though any good
christian had ever denied it. We may tell ourselves that
modern psychology has exploded God, having culled the
phrase from a book in the lending library; or that medie-
val mummery has no place in a stream-lined world—and
if this is true it is a pity, for people are all the better for an
element of carnival in their lives, but it is quite irrelevant.

And when we add on to this all the ordinary inhibi-
tions we all suffer from where thought is concerned—the

muddle-headedness, the absorption in the immediate and sensuous, the ability to persuade ourselves that we are exploring every avenue when in reality we are exploring every avenue but the right one—then we can realize the amount of preliminary spade-work that has to be done.

But now, suppose that we have done the spade-work, we really have an open mind, we really want to arrive at the truth, but none the less a really rational doubt about religion remains: what are we to do? If we begin at the very beginning we must ask: Is reasoning valid of reality in any case? And the sceptic within us may reply at once, no. If he does, he is guilty of self-contradiction. He has destroyed his case by asserting it: he has claimed the certitude which he is supposed to deny; and so he will have to begin with shame to take the lower place. More probably he will only say that it is probable that the answer is no; but again he is faced with grave difficulties; for if he *asserts* that it is probable he is again claiming certitude and denying his own scepticism, whereas if on the other hand he fails to assert that it is probable he is in fact abandoning his position. But the really entrenched sceptic (who lives deep down inside all of us) will remain unmoved by these arguments: he will go on repeating simply and dully, I don't know, to every question, even the question whether he is doubtful about his own doubt. In that case we must confront him with the principle of contradiction. He may say that to be or not to be is the question; what he cannot say, what it is quite meaningless to say, is that to be and not to be may be the same. If he really said that he held that proposition to be meaningful he would be mentally dead.

Now supposing that we have so far faced and vanquished our sceptical Shadow as to have found a sure basis for thinking, a possibility of at least some certitude, we cannot get far with the problem of God's existence without coming upon the idea of causality. And though we may feel sure that certitude about some things is possible, can we be sure that certitude about the validity of the idea of causality is possible? Here we may well be met by the somewhat desiccated ghost of the philosopher David Hume; who held that, since knowledge comes to us through the senses, and the senses introduce us only to singulars, all that we can in fact know is that certain phenomena tend to appear in a regular sequence. The weak point of such a position is that, though it holds that all our knowledge is sense-knowledge of particulars, it itself appeals not to the senses but to the reason. Fortunately we can go further than that, and find a more direct defence of the reality of causes; but first we ought to salute another ghost, Immanuel Kant, who held that causality is merely a mental category which the mind applies to phenomena but does not discover in or behind phenomena. To which the reply of Fichte seems to hold good, that there is no reason in that case why the mind should apply this category to this class of phenomena rather than to that; and moreover Kant is himself inconsistent since he allows that things are themselves the cause of sensation.

Can we then advance a more positive argument in defence of causality? We can: by returning to the principle of contradiction. The mind inevitably seeks causes. We see smoke, and look for fire; and our justification is this, that when a thing—or, if you prefer it, a group of phenomena,—changes, i.e. when it becomes what it was not before, we are forced to say either that the change is due to something else, a cause, or else that the thing in question had this new quality or state all the time: in other words that there has been change and yet not change, that to be and not to be are the same.

One can do no more here than touch on these steps in

the argument; and moreover if they appear extremely academic and unreal it is not surprising. We live in stark days. Discussion of the reality of causes is not for moments when lethal weapons are hurtling through the air; and lethal weapons, material and spiritual, are all too common in our world. But these things have to be mentioned for the argument to be complete; and we can now go on to more practical issues: the validity of the idea of causality once accepted, we can embark on the most fundamental of the arguments of St. Thomas for the existence of God: the one usually called the proof from movement.[1]

It would be better perhaps to say, from change. It is not physical motion particularly that is in question; which is why the value of the proof does not depend on physical science; any sort of change will do. Now if change implies a cause of the change, we soon find ourselves dealing with a string of causes. Let it be said at once that for the purposes of the argument we need to take a series of essentially subordinated causes which are all causing here and now in the present, not in a gradually receding time-series into the past. The possible eternity of the world, the possibility of an infinite multitude, these things are irrelevant. The wall becomes moist because the spout of the boiling kettle is up against it; the kettle boils because the fire heats the water; the fire heats the water because it is stoked up; you can prolong the series. What you cannot do is to prolong the series indefinitely if you want the kettle to boil. And so what the example shows us is this: that each cause only causes in so far as the one above it

---

[1] For a more detailed treatment of St. Thomas's proofs than was my purpose here, and in particular for a discussion of their validity in the light of later thought, such books as Garrigou-Lagrange: *God, His Existence and His Nature*, Phillips: *Modern Thomistic Philosophy*, may be consulted.

causes: and as you cannot go on for ever like that you must inevitably come to one that is not dependent on another higher one: you must come to an end one, that changes others but is not itself changed: you come to the unmoved Mover.

Now we must not at this point suppose that we have demonstrated the truth of the contents of the fourth Gospel: that we can never hope to do. But we have made a substantial advance; and we can go a good deal further. This first Mover is either changeable or unchangeable; if you say the former, you imply a changer, and in that case you will not have reached the first Mover at all. If on the other hand you say the latter, you are saying that the first Mover is unlimited: for every change implies the presence now of what was not there before, what was lacking before. The unchangeable is that to which nothing is lacking. But unlimited means infinite; and infinite means perfect; and perfect implies the presence of those attributes which are not merely perfections relative to a particular *kind* of being, like a pronounced ability to purr in a cat, but absolute perfections, though of course we can only know such perfections analogically as our own limited experience reveals them.

Thus we can come to predicate intellect of the first Cause; and since we must also predicate goodness and not evil, and since the pure intellectual apprehension of goodness produces love, we must also predicate love. The first Mover is also the first Knower and the first Lover: in other words is not an It but a He; and we stand on the threshold of the temple.

Now supposing that we accept that train of thought as valid, what sort of certainty have we gained from it? There is a certainty that attaches to statements like the principle of contradiction: and it is absolute certainty, because there is just no hope that it may conceivably not be so; and that is the kind of certainty which this proof produces, because it is based on precisely that sort of statement. But what we need to stress is this: that we might see that the thing in itself has that sort of certitude and yet we might not feel convinced: for it might well be that we had not so fully and deeply assimiliated it as to have that sort of certainty in a fully operative way, in all its practical cogency. We might say, I recognise that it is certain, absolutely certain, but somehow I don't feel overpowered by the evidence. And in that case it is possible to keep this purely rational assent locked away in the mind, as you put a letter away out of sight so as to forget to answer it.

That is why we need to go back to the point from which we started. Man is a rational *animal*. In these days especially, rational argument may not be enough. You can tell someone that his plain duty is to do this or that; and you can prove it to him by irrefragable logical argument; and at the end he will say, Yes I see, you're obviously right, but there the matter will rest.

When, therefore, you are arguing God's existence with your inner sceptic, there is no reason for surprise if you find that he accepts the force of your argument but is content to do nothing about it. The senses and emotions are meant to help us to God: and now is the time to draw on them.

There are other metaphysical arguments, of course; but there are other *kinds* of argument altogether, like the moral argument, and they may have more emotional pull on us. There are things like the testimony of mankind through the ages; and the more immediate and dramatic testimony of those very rational animals the mystics. Again, we shall not, unless we are very stupid, look to science either to prove or to disprove the existence of God; but science can lead us in the right direction; and there are valuable indications to be found, for instance, in the psychology of Jung; while one gathers that modern physics are more helpful in this respect than the Newtonian physics, which were too deeply embroiled with the philosophy of Descartes. All these may help; but these too are not enough.

The philosophical search for God is not complete without—and indeed is meant to lead up to—the search that has to go on in the heart. Rational knowledge is perfected when it becomes also love-knowledge; and that implies a personal relationship, and personal relationships are made and not born. You hear of some very thrilling and loveable personality, and you say, I must meet him: but you know that it will be a question of a very long process before you can say that you now know him. So it is with God; you have to get to know him, to realize gradually his presence in you and in the world, follow, at however respectful a distance, the mystics in their life of prayer, even if at the beginning you are more or less praying to the unknown God; and it is that journey out into the infinite Ocean that brings these philosophical discussions to life and makes them compelling: no longer a question of an abstract assent, but of being caught up with your whole being into the tempestuous energy and the searing love of the infinite consuming Fire. Train your senses to love the beauty of truth and goodness, not the shoddy and sham; try to make your emotional life the partner and not the rival of the life of the spirit: then you will acquire a greater directness and sureness of intellectual vision, and you will advance in wholeness and therefore with perfected certainty, because then you will know in your bones that God is not a remote abstraction in whose existence it is difficult to feel much intellectual confidence but an immediate and compelling presence, pressing in upon you on every side like the air you breathe, filling the tiniest object with the terrifying quality of immensity and the pathos of the condescension of infinite pity and love; and, in that awakening to the deepest reality of the world about you, your intellectual labours will have reached more than their immediate aim, which is rational certainty: they will have reached at least the outer confines of that ultimate kingdom which is the assumption of mind and heart alike into a sharing of the life of God.

Chapter 6: MORALITY AND HAPPINESS

The picture of man has led us to think of God, and of man's search for God, his plunge into the immensities of the Sea Pacific. But we cannot think of that search as an adventure remote from the humdrum events of everyday life: if we are ever to reach the fullness of life in God it must be through the way we live that everyday life, the way we use everyday events to become what it is our destiny to be. And so, at every turn, we find ourselves faced with the necessity of deciding whether we are to act in this way or in that: we find ourselves faced with the problem of morality. And about that problem it is very easy to be confused.

Let us start from the fact that, in questions of morality, people do have *reasons* for thinking that some things ought to be done and others not to be done. They may not always be good reasons; but at least they are reasons. The christian indeed does not always bother to think in terms of reasons: and sometimes that is very right and proper—with the very simple for instance—but sometimes it is not. A great deal of harm can be done by thinking and talking of the moral law as though it were a purely arbitrary *fiat*

on the part of God. For us, in this age and this environment, there are few things more important to be clear about
than this: that where the moral law is concerned, things are
not wrong because they are forbidden, but forbidden
because they are wrong. In other words, there is always a
very good *reason* for the moral imperative.

Why for instance do people think that murder or theft
or lying are wrong? Their conclusion may sometimes be
based on the recognition that actions of that sort are bound
to make social life, a reasonably placid social life, impossible. The line of argument is to be found for instance in
Hobbes's *Leviathan*. And if we feel that it does not go very
far we shall surely be right; but at least as far as it goes it has
an element of truth in it: it does provide a reason. It does
mean that you are not reduced to saying, I must not steal because if I do I shan't have my reward when the time comes.

If you run through the second table of the Law, the
last seven Commandments, you do find as a matter of fact
that if people ignore them social life does become impossible. If they pay no attention to their parents, refuse to
respect other people's lives and property, regard the break-
ing up of other families, other people's marriages, as a
legitimate pursuit, and have no scruple about defaming
their neighbours and doing violence to truth, then society
becomes chaotic, and life certainly becomes nasty and
brutish and probably short.

And the same line of argument applies to what at first
sight might be regarded as quite private and hidden mis-
demeanours. We may say, As long as I get drunk only
behind closed doors it does not affect the rest of the world;
but in reality it does, eventually. It affects the world because it affects us; it makes us persons of this sort rather
than of that; and therefore the effects of our contacts with
other people will be of this sort instead of that: they will be

harmful instead of beneficent, and they will help to make life coarse and disorderly instead of producing decorum and peace. We affect other people, and therefore society, by what we are.

But in saying all this one has already stated another reason for keeping the moral law; and a better one. It is not only that murder and so on make life in society uncomfortable: they degrade or destroy the sinner himself. A somewhat over-dramatized picture of that disintegration was provided by the painting of the sin-sodden Dorian Gray as the film presented it; and though the tendency is to think that that sort of thing is brought about only by certain kinds of vice, it seems true to say that on closer consideration all vices will be found to have that kind of effect, and the sins of the mind just as much as the sins of the body. We cannot lie or thieve, we cannot be cruel or covetous or cowardly or contemptuous, without disintegrating; and the things that these vices do to our bodies are signs of the things that they do to our souls, our whole personalities.[1]

But we can go further than this. The things which the commandments forbid are things which would be condemned in any case by any upholder of what we all agree, more or less, in regarding as an ideal for human nature. The world as a whole seems always to have held that a man ought to have certain qualities: he ought to be brave,

[1] It has to be noted that in the search for reasons it is no use examining an isolated incident. It is no use saying, I know water can't wear a hole in a rock because I've just seen a drop fall on a rock and it made no impression. It is no use saying, Yesterday I stole and it has made no impression: you have to look at a man who has stolen every day for the last twenty years, and see what it has done to *him*. He will probably by then be what we call a hardened sinner; and even if there were no other ill effect that would be quite enough: it means that he has gone hard, he has formed a carapace, and to that extent he has made himself less than a man.

strong-willed, large-hearted and generous, candid, trust-worthy, and so on; and the commandments say in effect that if you want to be like that you must act in this way and not in that.

And yet perhaps a difficulty presents itself. You might agree that this is so where it is a question of cruelty and injustice, of gross sensuality or the lust for power; but is it true of all the things the christian law condemns? And you might think of one particular example which is much in people's minds these days: the problem of contraception as it often presents itself today, when so often you find men and women who love each other deeply and want children, but, for economic reasons, let us say, are unable to have them. How can this prohibition be seen in the light of that search for the human ideal which we have been considering?

The answer surely is this. In the attempt to achieve the human ideal, as we have just been considering it, one might rightly recognize the aristotelean ethic or something very like it; and that ethic is a sound one and a noble one, and very reasonable. But, unless it is very carefully interpreted, it has, even as a natural ethic, a serious flaw in it. It lacks humility. It has intellectual modesty, the quiet virtues of the gentleman; but not humility of heart. It preaches man the master of his fate; and there is a sense of course in which christianity does the same—in the sense that we are to establish the rule of spirit over flesh, and to acquire the qualities of the virtuous life, by the exercise of our freedom. But we can only prevent man the master from becoming man the megalomaniac, we can only prevent the magnanimous man from becoming the proud man, by making quite sure that he knows he is also man the servant. We must sit down before the facts like a child, as T. H. Huxley put it: the humility of the scientist in face of the facts, the humility of the philosopher in face of the

truth: this has to be translated into terms of a general attitude to reality in the soul of everyman if nobility is not to
turn sour and disintegrate into pride. Humility in face of
the facts of reality, in face of the ultimate nature of things:
the religious man would say, in face of the nature of God.
Morality is the humble acceptance of, and obedience to,
absolute truth and absolute goodness: which means that
morality can never be true morality until it becomes
religion. Man can never be a master until he has learnt to
worship, to serve.

Let us put all that another way round. Aristotle tells us
the nature of man is this, and therefore the purpose of man's
life is that, and therefore you must act in such a way as to
achieve the purpose—you must learn to be wise, just,
strong, temperate. And all that is very true; but a great
deal depends on the motive. If you do as he says merely
because that is the way to become a perfect and therefore
happy man, you are in fact just being selfish. It may be an
exalted form of selfishness, so that often it is not recog-
nized as such; but it is selfishness none the less, because in
everything that you do you are acting ultimately for your
own sake. And there is in the human heart a deep conviction that selfishness is the very opposite of human perfection. What then is to be done about it? Is it a hopeless
vicious circle? No, the answer is quite simple.

Let us start from a fact. The fact is that we feel that selfishness is wrong quite apart from the consequences of
being selfish: we feel convinced that some things are right
and some wrong in themselves; and it naturally follows
that we ought to do the right and avoid the wrong not just
because of this or that consequence but absolutely. In other
words, it is part of human life—indeed it is the whole of
human life—to acknowledge, to worship and serve, absolutes, the absolutes of truth and goodness and beauty. The

true scientist does not acknowledge the facts only when they pay; the true philosopher does not claim to master truth but to love and serve it; the true man does not set out to adapt ultimate reality to himself but to adapt himself to ultimate reality.

And that is the third way in which there is a natural basis to the moral law: namely, that the moral law is precisely the natural law, the law of nature, the way reality is constituted. If you break the commandments it is bad for the peace and comfort of life in society: that is the first way. If you break the commandments it means the gradual disintegration of yourself as a human being: that is the second way. But also, if you break the commandments you are flouting the nature of reality, and there is an obstinate something within us that persists in telling us that that is a bad thing. If you drive a car in defiance of its nature you will not drive it far: and that is one good reason for not doing so. But quite apart from that, the whole idea of so using it, of doing violence to it, is intellectually repulsive. It is the same with the law of human nature. What we call the law of human nature is simply the pattern of ultimate reality as expressed in human nature. To be a man you have to worship that reality: you have to serve truth selflessly.

Let us return then to the problem of contraception. Is there any *reason* why it should be wrong in the sort of circumstances we were considering? The answer must be yes; because to be a man you have to reverence reality; and that means reverencing *all* reality: not just the big things, and certainly not just the grandiose abstractions, but the nature of all things, even the nature of your own organism and its functions. To pervert truth is an intellectual monstrosity; and to pervert a natural function is a way of perverting truth. And for that very reason it does become in the long run a disintegration of one's own personality; because in the long run you cannot make yourself master of reality, you cannot try to bend reality to your will regardless of its nature, without falling into the disintegration we call pride. You cannot try to become a god without becoming something less than a man.

Let us return for a moment to the beginning. Some people might condemn murder and the rest on hobbesian grounds; but no doubt the vast majority would not be bothered with all that reasoning; they would say in effect what we have just been saying: that there was something wrong about the things in themselves. In this country people do not quote Hobbes very much nowadays; what they do still say sometimes of an action they regard as wrong in itself is that it is not cricket. (Perhaps they think that that *is* something to do with Hobbes.) They are then putting in poetic form rather what Kant put more philosophically in terms of duty for duty's sake. And this theory too leaves something to be desired. It fails to satisfy because there is something about it ineradicably cold and impersonal. To worship an abstraction may be noble but it is not very comfortable; and it may be doubted whether for the ordinary run of men it is practicable. It will work for some things, where our emotions are engaged—love of country, for instance, or hatred of cruelty—but hardly so well in cases where we cling to the abstract ideal only with our reason. The abstract is often hard put to it to wean us from the immediate glamour of the concrete. And that leads us to the fourth way in which there is a natural basis of the moral law.

Morality is not true morality at all unless it becomes religion. That is true first of all in the sense we have already been thinking of: you cannot be a man without humility, without learning to sit down like a child in face of reality, without worshipping something greater than man. But there is a second sense; and it is this that redeems us from the chilly correctness of the idea of duty for duty's sake.

For us who are christians, truth is not an abstraction. Truth is God, and God is love. We are meant to try to serve God the Truth, not merely or ultimately for the sake of the paradise of God but for the sake of the God of paradise: we become fully men, so we believe, in so far as we more and more come to serve God simply from the motive of love. That motive does not necessarily exclude the others we have been considering; but it overtops them, and it redeems them of their weaknesses, and in the end it makes them seem very unimportant. Love does not look for reasons for loving. That is why to say, I must do this because God says so and that's enough, *may* indeed imply a wrongheaded and puerile attitude to religion, it *may* imply the belief that things are wrong simply and solely because they are (arbitrarily) forbidden, but on the other hand it may be the fullness of wisdom and life: it may mean that the self cannot think of acting otherwise because it is caught up through the power of love into the infinite life of God and that when it acts it is simply expressing that infinite life; it may mean that it acts as it does because it could say with St. Paul, I live, now not I, but Christ liveth in me. So it will be wise and just and strong and temperate; but it will be these things, not simply because it sees in them the only way to achieve its own greatness or happiness, nor yet because of a cold impersonal realization of the claims of the absolute, but as a lover singing his love, living his love.

But this, it might be said, is talking mysticism: this is a long way from the natural basis of the moral law. No, it is true that if we had not been shown the possibility of this destiny we should not have been able to guess it; but none the less there are two ways in which it fulfils the basic needs of our nature and is in that sense rooted in our nature even while it transcends it.

First, in the depths of human nature there is the desire to be happy. And naturally speaking we are in a dilemma. The one way in which to fail to be happy is to spend our time looking for happiness, as every practical hedonist finds out sooner or later; on the other hand, to try to keep the moral law not from self-regarding motives but from devotion to an impersonal absolute is, as we have seen, a chilly affair which is far from expressing our ideal of happiness. Yet there is no third way except the way of love: the love that fulfils the whole law, fulfils it in humility towards what is greater than man, because it has learnt that what is greater than man is not an It but a He, a personal God more loveable than all the loveliness of the world. You can be happy only when you love; you can be totally happy only when you love the All with all your being—when you love God with all your heart and soul and strength.

What then is the natural basis of the moral law in this its fullness? Simply this, in the first place, that only thus can you be happy because only thus can you love infinity and be filled with it. To say, I must do this because it is the way to be happy: that is an answer that meets the deep demands of human nature; and now you can give that answer without falling into a vicious circle, because now you can define happiness in a way that transcends the selfish.

And the second answer really does no more than state the same thing in a deeper, simpler and more direct way. Morality becomes fully itself when it becomes religion; but religion has its natural basis in man's natural desire for God, and therefore morality shares the same basis. Morality *is* the means whereby the self is brought gradu-

A.H.

ally into conformity with the divine life, and therefore is the means whereby the desire for God is both expressed and fulfilled. Let us recall what St. Augustine has to say of the inescapable yearning of the human heart for God; of what St. Thomas tells us of the same natural desire; and let us recall also the old scholastic adage, that if you will the end you necessarily will also the means to the end —and the means to God is morality in its fullness as a life of love and worship.

What natural grounds are there then for accepting and obeying the moral law? There are four. First, because otherwise social life is impossible; and that is a sound reason, though not very exalted if you are thinking of your own comfort. Secondly, because otherwise you cannot be fully a man, you will disintegrate; and that too is a sound reason and a strong one, though to make it thoroughly valid you have to free it of its egoism, which can be done by going on to the next reason. Thirdly then, because truth is an absolute and absolutes must be served for their own sake: the nature of reality, in all its manifestations, must be respected; and that again is a strong answer, though it lacks appeal to the heart unless we carry it on to the fourth point. Fourthly, because the absolute is in fact the God who is love, and who alone can fully draw and satisfy the human heart, so that only by serving his law out of love can we be true not only to his nature but to our own. So in this fourth reason all the others are resumed and perfected; and so it is that we are told that love is the fulfilment of the law.

Let us clinch the matter finally by recalling St. François de Sales and his partridges. Although human nature, he says, is gravely depraved by sin, yet the sacred inclination to love God above all things has remained in us. . . . With partridges it often occurs that some steal the eggs of others in order to brood; ... and it is a strange but well-attested fact that when the chick hatched and nourished under the wing of the thievish partridge first hears the cry of the true mother ... it forthwith quits the thievish partridge and hurries to meet and follow its own parent. ... Thus, Théotime, it is with our heart; for although hatched, nourished and brought up among things temporal, low and transitory ... yet at the first look it casts towards God, at the first consciousness inspired by him, the natural inclination to love him, slumbering and imperceptible till now, awakes in an instant unawares, as a spark among ashes, and affecting the will, gives it an impulse of the supreme love due to the sovereign and first Principle of all things.

And again the same saint tells us that our hearts are like stags adorned by great princes with collars bearing their arms; for the natural desire of the heart for God is a secret token that we belong to him.

Signatum est saper nos lumen vultus tui: the light of his countenance is signed upon us; and reason, which is of the stuff of our nature, is called the candle of the Lord; or again, as the men of prayer so often tell us, the spirit of man is as a spark thrown off by the infinite Fire; and that is why there is no rest for it until it find rest in the heart of the Fire, and no happiness for it until it is at least on the way back, the way of morality, the way we call the growth to holiness or wholeness.

The moral law is rooted in our nature by more than the desire we have for social tranquillity, by more than the desire to see the humanist values fully vindicated and the humanist ideal achieved, by more than the conviction that lies deep in us, clouded often but never extinguished, that our nature cannot fashion truth for itself but must accept and acknowledge and serve it. The heart of man is a flame that of itself soars upwards; that being low, and knowing its lowness, longs to be lifted on high; and that upward striving, supported by the arms of God, is what we mean by the moral law: not a static conforming to a static code, but a growth into the rhythm of infinite life. Duty for duty's sake has of itself something dreary about it, the endless weary plodding along the level plain. But this, this is duty for love's sake; you leave the horizontal for the vertical; you soar into regions where sorrow can be turned, not hereafter but now, into joy; and nature, hardened and immobilized by sin, can be thawed and energized into liberty of movement, and find its blindly desired fulfilment: for this love is its life and its strength and its blessedness, the fulfilment of the heart's desire.

Chapter 7: WHAT THINK YE OF CHRIST?[1]

The universe is bent and twisted: you look about the world, and the picture of man we have been considering seems no more than an empty dream, a wish-fulfilment, mocked at by the reality we know. But christianity has no illusions about the condition of man; it has no reason to try to minimize the fact of sin; on the contrary, it paints the picture with a starkness which is all that the most hard-headed realist could desire; only, it then goes on to say that this is not the final thing, that darkness can be redeemed and turned into light, that death can be turned into life; but that this can be done only in the power of him who said, I am the Way and the Truth and the Life— the Christ, the Son of God.

We must go on then to consider the problem which confronts so many today, so many perhaps who do

[1] In this chapter I am particularly indebted to Karl Adam: *The Son of God*, and Léonce de Grandmaison, S.J.: *Jesus Christ*, vol. 2.

believe in God and love him and try to serve him, but who
cannot see their way to go on to a full acceptance of the
christian faith: can we really believe that the Gospel story
is true, and that Christ is God?

We have been thinking of the necessity, in studying any
such problems as these, of having a really open mind, of
being on the alert for, and refusing to be swayed by, emotional reactions or prejudices or defence mechanisms; of
being ready to say, I will follow the clue wherever it leads,
even though it plays havoc with my sense of security or my
comfort or my sloth. That is true of any such problem; it
is especially true of the problems of God's existence and
Christ's divinity, for they put quite special demands on
us. We know that one cannot hope to demonstrate the
divinity of Christ as one demonstrates a mathematical
theorem; but to be openminded is to realize that an inves-
tigation may lead to the point at which the only reasonable thing to do is to pray for the gift of faith. And in that
case to open the mind is not enough: we have to open the
heart. The hunger for the Infinite is in all of us, and therefore, when the Infinite manifests itself it calls forth a
special response from us: a total response. Not merely the
mind, but the emotions, the heart, the will, are involved;
and so we have to be prepared to follow the clue in that
sense too: we have to be prepared to say, If this does lead
to the threshold of the Infinite, and I find there a challenge
to change the whole direction and texture of my life, I'll
accept the challenge.

And this must come about, not merely the first time we
embark on this inquiry, but every time. We may already
believe; but here on earth we see, as St. Paul tells us, only
in part, we have dark glimpses as in a glass; and each time
we look with real care and humility and effort we may
glimpse a little more; and then the challenge widens and

deepens and there is need of a wider and deeper response: we may have to arrange our lives anew all over again. We need to begin the inquiry with prayer; we shall certainly need to end it in prayer.

What is the personality that the Gospels reveal to us? In these days we need no longer give anxious consideration to those theories, popular some years ago, which sought to prove by eviscerating the text of the Gospels that only what was called the historic Christ existed at all: a man from whom all awkward supernaturalisms had been removed. That line of criticism ended, finally, in the assertion that this historic Christ never existed at all. Nowadays no scholar doubts the substantial authenticity of the Gospel narrative;[1] and we can therefore search it as a whole for the portrait we need.

Nor need we be delayed by other unworthy shifts and subtleties. There are some who have held that our Lord began as a good and humble servant of Jahweh but was led astray in the end, ambition feeding on the adulation of disciples and crowd, till he thought he was indeed the equal of God. There is not the slightest ground in the Gospel story for any such theory: our Lord begins, as a child, by proclaiming the supremacy of his Father's will and his Father's business, and it is equally to the Father that he commits himself at the end when the work is done; and if we want the most striking instances of his humility and gentleness we shall find them, not in the early Galilean ministry, but at the end, when he washes his disciples' feet at the Supper and is silent before Herod's mockery and only prays for those who crucify him. At no time was there any shred of arrogance in the man who ate with the lowly and the sinful, and who refused to condemn the woman they wanted to stone. And of the shameful and

[1] Cf. Sir Frederick Kenyon: *Our Bible and the Ancient Manuscripts.*

sordid suggestion which impugns our Lord's mental balance we need only recall that even Renan dismissed it with scorn.

No, there are two alternatives, and no more. Jesus' own ideas about himself are clear; and either he was right, or else he was a tragically misguided visionary. We must see which of the two alternatives is the more likely in the light of his personality.

The human mind works *dividendo et componendo*: and it is useful, if one is trying to understand something, to examine its two most contradictory features and then search for a clue which will weld them into a unity. Let us start then with the two apparently most contradictory elements in our Lord's personality. He said of himself, The Father is greater than I. He also said: The Father and I are one; and, Philip, he that has seen me has seen God. And throughout his ministry, from the very beginning to the very end, you find words and actions which express the one thought or the other. What is the clue that unites them?

Let us begin at the beginning. There is no doubt among his contemporaries, there is no doubt in the Gospels, that Jesus was true man. We learn a good deal, first of all, about his physical qualities. He must have had great external charm, if you think of the way children loved him and those in trouble of any sort ran to him. He must have been very strong and virile: he rises very early to pray, and often spends the night in prayer as well; in any case he has often nowhere to sleep but the open air. Throughout the years of his ministry he is always journeying on foot, and with the simplest provisions; sometimes he is kept by the sick till very late in the evening and has no time to eat. He has to cope with the vast crowds that press upon him; he has to be alert for the controversial attacks of his enemies; his closest disciples are often a trial to his patience because of their inability to understand and their narrowness of outlook. Only the healthiest and strongest physique could have remained uninjured; and we are told that our Lord's last journey from Jericho to Jerusalem, through rocky country and under a broiling sun, involved a climb of 3500 feet or so in six hours—and it was after that that he took part in the banquet at Bethany given by Lazurus and his sisters.

And what of the mind of Jesus? Writers have pointed with justice to its clarity and assurance as the things that stand out most strikingly. He knows—and from boyhood he knew—exactly what he is and what his mission is; you notice the number of times he says, I am come for this or that purpose, I am not come for this other. And because he sees so clearly, there is never any hint of uncertainty, of vacillation, of compromise. Let your speech, he says, be Yea, yea and Nay, nay; and his own words always have that directness and candour and genuineness.

The same is true when he is stern and angry. People sometimes think that this harshness is out of keeping with the gentleness of Christ; in fact it is part of the same thing; a love of humanity, as Chesterton pointed out, implies a hatred of inhumanity; a perfect vision and love of the truth implies a hatred of deceit and falsehood. If you water down love into a romantic emotion, and goodness into a mild sentimental kindliness, then of course anger seems out of place. We need to remember that love is terrible; that in the *Paradiso* Beatrice makes Dante cry; and that anger may be not a vice but a duty, when it is as clear and controlled and selfless as was Christ's.

There is the same clarity of vision, the same control of every situation, in the logic with which our Lord meets and beats the heckling of Pharisee and Sadducee on their own ground; and again, still more strikingly perhaps, in the way he refuses, and refuses with quiet assurance, to be deflected in any way from his purpose by those who love him. And, of course, clarity of mind implies realism. Christ lives for his fellow-men, and dies for his fellow-men; but he is never blind to their faults, their stupidities, their vices, the terrible weight of malice and hatred and stark evil that is in the world. You could not imagine anything more remote from a highflown idealism. Love of humanity in the abstract is all too often compatible with hatred or contempt for real men and women; our Lord has no illusions about the world, it is a wicked and adulterous generation, but there is no parallel to his gentleness and his pity where there is suffering and weakness and the first faint flicker of sorrow for sin and love for God in the heart. You remember the publican in the parable; the woman taken in adultery; our Lord's gentleness with Peter after the denial, and with Judas too after the betrayal.

And as you consider the heart of Christ, notice his love for the small things of life, the value he gives them. He knew the roads and fields and waters of Palestine, because he spent his days and nights in them; and he loves them and can bring them to life in his stories. He loves the small people; and they too are as vivid in his tales as the kings and the rich men. The sublimity of the Last Supper discourse is not contradictory but complementary to the simplicity of the parables or the anger of the denunciations: these things together express the personality which, in its prophetic vision, can fuse eternity and time into one, and in its love of the real world can find nothing too unimportant for its notice and its care.

In all this human side of our Lord the one note is dominant: I must be about my Father's business; Pray to your Father; Why dost thou call me good? None is good but God; The Father is greater than I. It is the Father, and the will and the work of the Father, that matter. Jesus is the servant of Jahweh.

And yet there is the other side. He that sees me sees God; Behold a greater than Solomon here; I tell you there is here a greater than the Temple; The Son of Man is Lord of the Sabbath; He that loveth father and mother more than me is not worthy of me; No one knoweth the Son but the Father, neither doth anyone know the Father but the Son; I am the Bread of Life; I am the Way and the Truth and the Life; Before Abraham was made, I am. You cannot fail to see in that last phrase the assumption of eternity, the echo of the name of God. And you notice, at the end, when the witnesses at the trial cannot agree, and Caiaphas is driven to questioning our Lord himself and adjures him by the living God, so that he must as a Jew give an answer, his answer is as quiet and unequivocal in tone as it is world-shaking in meaning: I *am* the Son of the Blessed One, and you shall see the Son of Man coming in clouds of glory . . .

You remember other things: the changing of the Mosaic law on his own authority; the healing and raising to life on his own authority—I will, be thou made clean; the forgiving of sin, on his own authority; you remember the immense demands he makes on men, the equality he claims with God; and yet this is the humble man of Galilee, the lover of the small things, beloved of the small and poor and weak; the man who, for all his physical strength, could be weary, for all his intellectual mastery could be sad even unto death.

What then is the clue that binds these apparent contradictions into a single unbreakable unity? We shall find it if we think a little of his *prayer*. There are two things to be noted. First, this man, who can speak to such purpose about pride and evil and sin, and the fear of sin, never once betrays any hint of a personal sense of sin, never once expresses any sense of the infinite remoteness of man from the infinite purity of God. And yet with other holy men it is on these things that their holiness is based. Secondly, his prayer is a thing in which not even his closest disciples normally share; he goes to a place apart; it is his secret life with his Father. And you notice how this separateness from other men is expressed: Thus you shall pray, he says, *Our* Father; but for himself it is never Our Father, it is always *My* Father. And when he speaks to his disciples he makes the same thing clear, the same distinction, Your Father, My Father. For other men there must be awe and fear and penitence, the prayer of the publican; for Jesus there is only the sense of intimate loving communion, a communion unbroken by the spiritual crises and upheavals you find in other great men of prayer, a sense of oneness which is with him from the beginning to the end.

Jesus is true man; and having human nature he must, like other men, pray to God. But what is special, what is unique about this prayer supplies the clue to the apparent contradictions in his character. What can harmonize the obvious humility and gentleness of the man with the arrogance of his demands, the arrogance of *I* am the Way, Come to *me,* He that sees *me* sees God? What can harmonize the intense sympathy, the co-suffering with sinners, with the claim to be Judge of living and dead? What can harmonize the utter dependence on and obedience to the Father with the assumption of unconditioned authority and absolute claims? You find the answer in the prayer of Christ because there you find, not a split personality, for nothing could be more alien to the constant and steadfast grip on reality and truth which is so obvious in Christ, but a person who knows that there must be worship and prayer and dependence because there is a human nature; but who knows also at the same time that it is never a human nature which prays and is dependent but a person, and that there the person is not on a level with the human nature but with the nature of God. The nature is possessed by the person, and so there is no sin nor sense of sin, no diffidence, no fear, before the face of God. The nature is possessed by the person: and so there is no arrogance in the simple statement of the person's supremacy and rights, and no contradiction between them and the lowliness of the nature in which all humanity's sufferings are gathered and offered to God. And when the prophetic vision of Christ fuses the long procession of time into the immediate now of eternity, and reveals himself as simultaneously saviour and judge, it is again only because the nature of man who is bound by time is possessed by the personality which is beyond time.

When you realize that this is indeed Infinity assuming all the reality of a finite nature, the Word indeed becoming flesh, then you realize that without these apparent contradictions there would have been only a partial, a one-sided statement; we should have seen the God or the man, but not the God-man. And the reverse is true; for once you rule out—as the compelling evidence makes you rule out —the possibility of a tragic self-deception on the part of an unbalanced mind, there is only the one conclusion: there is here a man who speaks with consistency and mastery and the calm that comes of perfect comprehension, and who speaks alike as God and as man, and who combines in the unsoundable depths of his personality the qualities expressed by his words. We are left, like the centurion, to conclude, Truly this was the Son of God.

But there is a final possibility of mental withdrawal from this conclusion, and we ought to look at it. Especially in these days, we dislike being driven into something too definite. Might it not be, we think, that all this is true enough provided we leave it sufficiently hazy, sufficiently buried in the ambiguity of mystery? The evidence is indeed that Christ was both human and divine; but could he not somehow be divine without actually being God? What a mass of dogma, what a pressure of claim and challenge, that supposition would free us from . . . But if we take refuge there we are ignoring the whole historical setting of these historical events. We cannot put the presuppositions of Greek polytheism into a mind whose whole background was purely Hebrew and therefore purely monotheist. Our Lord was born into a society which knew the one true God; to that belief he subscribed all his life. The thing is clear-cut: either he was one with Jahweh, or, for all his graces, he was purely man. To say anything different is to say once again that he was deluded: and we are not only back again at the incompatibility of such delusions with the clarity and limpidity of his mind, but we are also set the quite insoluble problem of how any such idea of shared divinity could ever have occurred to him. The paradoxes remain: I am one with the Father, I am less than the Father; and the one solution remains, I am a person possessing equally two separate natures, finite and Infinite. The personality of Jesus revealed in the Gospels leads us to the affirmations of the Creeds and the Councils.

We must return then to the thought of the response this inquiry demands of us. Man is a hunger for the Infinite, and where the Infinite is manifested the whole man must respond. This is a man who not only makes clear his own status, but makes equally clear demands. And he said to them, Come after me. . . . and *immediately* leaving their nets they followed him. It is as total a self-giving as that; it is the potter with his clay. If we shy from that conclusion we are being untrue to our own minds. In one way or another the same call comes to us in our turn from the Gospel pages: and in one way or another we must be prepared to leave our nets immediately, absolutely, finally, without reserve.

And last of all, when we think to whom we are asked to give this total allegiance and loyalty, we must remember the whole portrait: He that sees me sees God; in Christ there is the infinite gentleness of God but there is also the infinite purity; there is not only the loveliness, there is the terror, of love. Both together must condition our response and give urgency to our obedience: for us the joy, but only if first the sense of sin, the sorrow. You remember *The Wind in the Willows,* when the two animals, Rat and Mole, come to the island where the Presence is:

Rat, he found breath to whisper, shaking. Are you afraid?

Afraid, murmured the Rat, his eyes shining with unutterable love. Afraid! Of *Him?* O, never, never! And yet—and yet—O, Mole, I am afraid.

Chapter 8: DOGMA AND FREEDOM

Suppose now that you have come to the point at which you are prepared in mind and heart to accept the claims of Christ, prepared to accept his teaching and obey his commands: is there anything to prevent your becoming formally a christian? The answer might well be, Yes, the Church. You might feel that the personality and teaching of Christ were one thing, the formal dogmas of the Church and its claim to infallible teaching authority quite another. Yet for the christian the Church is indeed, despite the sins and stupidities and betrayals of the human beings who make it up, the continuation of the life of Christ on earth, wielding his authority, imparting his truth, conveying his life and his power to men. Behold, he had said to his followers, I am with you all days even to the consummation of the world. And to Peter: Feed my lambs, feed my sheep. Does the Church in fact speak with the voice of Christ; or is it a merely human attempt to tyrannize over the minds of other men? Can there be compatibility between an acceptance of infallible dogmas and the free service of Christ? It is these things that we must next consider.

It is important at the outset to be clear about what the catholic view of the matter is. For the catholic, you misunderstand the Church sadly unless you see its teaching authority, not as a denial of thought, but as an invitation to thought; not as that which makes constructive thinking impossible, but as that which makes it possible. Can that view be justified?

During the war, when the signposts were removed from the countryside, we found that setting out for a destination meant going far but not necessarily arriving anywhere. It is the same with the mind. The boy they discovered recently who had been brought up by a herd of gazelles can run, but there is no evidence that he can think. To be able to think for ourselves we need to be taught. When you are very young you take what is told you with placid confidence; a little older, you discredit *a priori* the sayings of some of the more unpleasing classes of society: parents, schoolmasters, clergymen; a little older still and you widen the area of unbelief to include the rest of mankind. But if you stay indefinitely there you run the risk of killing your mind: you tend to flounder and then to disintegrate; and you may all too easily end up, as Aristotle would say, a *phuton*, a cabbage.

The fact is that the soul like the body will wither and

die unless it is nourished from without; if you want to go on living and growing you have to emerge from your splendid isolation and acquire humility and end up by saying—to Aristotle, to Plato, to somebody or another—that he is a better and wiser man than you.

But of course you ask from your teacher, not ready-made answers to every question, but the sort of sense of direction which will enable you to tackle the questions. And that must mean that you take as your teacher only the man who can convince you, in the deepest level of your mind, of the truth of his fundamental principles, his ultimate attitude to reality, and whose teaching therefore, at the deepest level, satisfies your own mind.

It was so that men came to Christ. Master, they said to him, thou hast the words of life. And they followed him. It did not mean that with him they felt they would never need to think again, but that with him they felt their thinking and their living would be along the right lines. The Church, in its claims to magisterial authority, also claims that. It claims that and no more; and could it, without ceasing to be Christ's Church, claim less? And would it, if it did, do a service or a disservice to the thought of mankind? Those are the two questions we have to consider.

First of all let us briefly rehearse the traditional doctrine. What does infallibility mean? It is not revelation: the imparting of some new and hitherto unknown truth. It is not inspiration, whereby the biblical writer is guided as to what to put down or omit, like a pen in the hand of the holy Spirit. It is not, most emphatically, impeccability, which means the inability to sin, a quality no man can claim this side beatitude. Infallibility is a negative thing: an inability to make mistakes; but an inability to make mistakes within a very narrow sphere. Go and teach all nations whatsoever things I have commanded you, said our Lord; but those things were concerned only with what we call faith and morals: what we should believe about God and ultimate reality, and how we should act in view of those beliefs.

But there are further restrictions to be made. When is this voice of certainty to be heard? Only in three cases. There is the ordinary *magisterium,* as it is called, of the Church: the *de facto* unanimity of all the bishops, each teaching his own flock; but this is usually hard to gauge. There is the oecumenical council, in which the assembled bishops under the leadership of the Pope promulgate a doctrine in the name of the holy Spirit. There is finally the Pope himself when speaking as the head of the whole Church, to the whole Church, with the intention of making a definitive doctrinal pronouncement.

And what kinds of truth can be comprised under the heading of faith and morals? Primarily, the things that have been formally revealed by God; secondarily, the things that are so bound up with these that error about them would involve error about the primary truths: of this sort are theological conclusions, as they are technically called, conclusions deduced from one revealed and one non-revealed premiss; or dogmatic facts, such as that a certain proposition is in fact contained in a given book; or again the sort of truths which enshrine teaching about the ideal of christian living.

And in all these cases the infallibility is restricted to the particular words or sentences in which it is clearly the intention of Pope or Council to *make* an infallible pronouncement: the few essential words of encyclical or bull for example, not the arguments or historical surveys which may lead up to them.

Further, we believe not in a creed but through a creed.

A.H

We believe in God; but God is ineffable; the most that human speech can do is to try to approximate in some way to reality through the use of our all too earthy symbols. Historically, the dogmatic truths have been couched in terms of a particular sort of philosophy; but that does not mean that the philosophy itself is divinely guaranteed; it only means that the use of its terms in order to clothe revealed reality is guaranteed.

And that leads us to the last and most important restriction. Infallibility is mainly a defensive thing: coming into play when the truth revealed by Christ is in danger of being denied or perverted or misunderstood. The great affirmation that Mary is the Theotokos, the Mother of God, was necessary to defend the divinity of her Son; the definition of the Immaculate Conception was necessary to preserve the universality of Christ's redemption. It becomes clear how far we are from the bull-on-the-breakfast-table mentality: the idea that the Pope should at frequent intervals produce a new and hitherto unventilated doctrine to add to the body of christian teaching. And when you say that infallibility is mainly defensive, you reach the great central truth of the matter: it is the Church as a whole that is infallible; it is the Church as a whole of which Christ the Truth said, Behold I am with you all days even to the consummation of the world: it is the Church as a whole to which he promised to send the Paraclete, the Spirit of Truth.

That leads us on to the ordinary way in which even the magisterial exercise of infallibility arises. What is the normal course of events? The normal thing is that gradually a dogma comes to be acknowledged and asserted in the devout life, the prayer-life, of the faithful. The theologians then, as the next stage in the process, investigate the validity of this new development and its doctrinal implications. The third stage comes when these discussions tend, as is the case with most human disputes, to lead to an exaggeration of relative positions, until in the end one or the other side comes near to damaging a more primary truth, a truth already guaranteed. Then the last stage is reached: the authoritative voice decides the matter finally; as Augustine said long ago, *Roma locuta est, causa finita est.*

But when you say *causa finita est,* do you mean *cogitatio finita est* also, do you mean that thought is killed? On the contrary, you mean that with a more sure sense of direction the work can now go on. Milton painted with fiery eloquence the horrors of censorship, the beneficent effects of freedom of thought and of pen; and where all too fallible civil authorities are concerned he was surely, in general, on the right lines; but where the possibility of a divine guidance is concerned we might judge a little by results. Some of his finest lines describe the city of freedom, the mansion house of liberty: the shop of warre hath not there more anvils and hammers waking, he says,. . . than there be pens and heads there, sitting by their studious lamps, musing, searching, revolving new notions and ideas . . . , others as fast reading, trying all things, assenting to the force of reason and convincement. If his argument were right this should be the very opposite of the picture presented by the Church; but is it? On the contrary, this *is* the picture of the Church's life: the years, the centuries go by, and sometimes, it is true, you come into the doldrums where little is produced but what has been said, and perhaps said better, before; but these periods are transient, and the great story of unfolding truth goes on: the searching, the trying, go on; and year by year and century by century the human mind advances always a little further into the understanding of the infinity of God.

Could the Church claim less? We can answer best by

looking at the alternative. It is possible indeed to make a
very attractive picture of the christian search for truth
along evolutionary lines: entirely free and independent,
we each discover what we can and, though even about
essentials it may be either right or wrong, we put it forth;
and as the ages go by, out of the clash of truth and falsehood
the reality emerges and grows, the Spirit remotely guiding
this dialectic process, until in the end humanity reaches
the fullness of truth. It is an attractive theory at first sight;
but there are major objections to it.

In the first place it fails to represent the mind and purpose of Christ. The words are clear: I am the Truth: go
and teach what I have commanded you. The revelation
is given; it is a treasure to be guarded and preserved, the
gates of hell shall not prevail against it. And there are the
terrible sanctions imposed: He that believeth not shall be
condemned: and would such sanctions be set by the God
of love against disbelief in what might well be false? Our
Lord was not planning to give his brother-men the life-
bringing truth in some remote age when the frailties of the
human mind might at last have arrived at it. I *am* the Way
and the Truth: here and now; you have what is necessary
now and for ever. Development there must be, yes; but
development is not evolution: the essentials are there,
given, clear.

Secondly, we return to the judgement by results. Is
absence of all guidance really better, really more inducive
to constructive work? Is it not rather the fact that the refusal of authority and the assertion of untrammelled private
judgement have led in fact to a state of affairs in which, as
Reinhold Niebuhr put it, the attempt to accommodate
religion to the modern mind ended in capitulation to its
thin soul?

Thirdly, we completely distort the picture of the Church

if we think of it exclusively in terms of an intelligentsia. There are other things in the world besides musing heads and pens. Our Lord told Peter: Feed my lambs, feed my sheep. Feed my lambs: there are all the simple and un-lettered, all those who are not capable of deep theological thinking; and they are the Body of Christ; and they look for the truth to those who represent Christ and his promise of the truth; they need to be led if they are not to go astray; and how shall they be led aright if every shepherd points them a different way?

How could the Church claim less? If you once accept the fact that Christ is God made man, who came to teach men the truth and whose will it was to build a Church not merely to carry on his work but to be as it were a con-tinuation of himself, his own mystical Body, his power and his life flowing through it and animating it: if you accept all this as you find it in the Gospel, then surely you have already accepted the idea that that Body must at least be so far preserved from error as to keep the essentials of his teaching intact. For there is only one alternative: that the Church which is the *totus Christus,* the Church which is vivified by Christ, should yet be able to fall so far away from him as to teach the opposite of what he taught; and that alternative is surely inadmissible.

But there are some who would admit that the Church must be able to speak with authoritative and certain voice, but who cannot accept the personal infallibility of the Pope, which they regard as a dogma invented by the Vatican Council in 1870. It was indeed amid the crash of thunder and the flash of lightning at the end of that Council that the dogma was defined, the rows and rows of assembled bishops at length registering their *placet*; and it is worth recalling that it *was* at length, for there had been a battle; but the great majority of those who opposed the definition opposed it on grounds of expediency only, and those few who opposed it on doctrical grounds were concerned with the question of the extent to which the Pope should previously consult the Church. For indeed the Scriptures, here if anywhere, are clear. Thou art Rock, and upon this Rock I shall build my Church; and there is that other passage, with its dramatic change from plural pronoun to singular, when Christ says to Peter: Behold Satan hath desired to have you that he might sift you as wheat; but I have prayed for thee, that thy faith fail not; and thou, being once converted, confirm thy brethren. And through the succeeding ages the doctrinal supremacy of Rome is again and again made clear: Peter has spoken through Leo, Peter has spoken through Agatho, the formulas run; and the fourteenth century Council of Florence only makes fully explicit the doctrine which has been acted upon throughout the Church's history.

There are indeed a few well-thumbed historical objections to be dealt with. There is Pope Liberius, who is said to have subscribed to an Arian creed and to have condemned Athanasius: to which the answer is given that in fact it is doubtful which creed he subscribed to, and that he did not condemn Athanasius for heresy. There is Pope Honorius who is accused of teaching the heresy of monothelitism and of having been condemned by an oecumenical Council: in fact his intention seems to have been, not to teach at all, but to allay the bitternesses of controversy, and he was censured not for being unorthodox himself but for not having quashed heresy in others. Finally there is of course the question, What of Galileo? But Galileo was condemned not by the Pope but by a Roman Congregation; and the Congregations are not infallible and have never claimed to be.

No, the real difficulty does not lie in these historical

points; it lies much more, in the last resort, in the nature of man. We dislike having things too clearly defined. We are ready enough to admit that the Spirit guides the Church and keeps its faith intact in a general sort of way; but the idea that you can point to a particular set of words, drawn up by a particular man, and say, These are true and beyond cavil and irreformable: that is a very different thing: and you have to make something more than an intellectual inquiry, you have to make an act of will before you can overcome the reluctances of the emotional level, the independence, the dislike of being pinned down.

And that is why, with this as with so many other catholic dogmas, everything depends on the angle of approach. If you look at these things in isolation from their context, their background, and as though from outside, then they can indeed look wildly improbable. But if you see them within the framework of the continued Christ-life on earth, a Christ-life that you have learnt not only to assess with your mind but to love and revere in your heart, then they may well look not improbable but inevitable. And this surely is the case with the present question. You think of the love of Christ the Truth wanting his lambs to be fed with that truth till the consummation of time: and what can that mean but that the Peter of today, whether alone or with his bishops in council, should be able to defend the truth with unerring voice, or guide with unerring hand the unending efforts of christians to see deeper and deeper into the things of God. The Church is the continuing Christ-life on earth: it is to the Church that we in our generation can go, as in Palestine two thousand years ago they went to Christ, and can say to it as they said to him, Master, thou hast the words of life.

PART FOUR

Applications

Chapter 9: COME, LIVE WITH ME

Religion, we have seen, is not something contrasted with the everyday business of living; it is a way of living, it is the fullness of living, that life of everyday. And that means two things. It means first of all that christianity does not merely accept the facts of human life while leaving them unchanged; does not merely bless the facts of human life while leaving them unchanged: it adds something to their very nature; it enhances them, deepens and enriches them even *as* human experience. So it is worth our while to look at some of the most important and precious of human experiences, and to try to see something of this process of enrichment in them. But in the second place we can remember the saying of our Lord, By their fruits ye shall know them: and we can look at these things with that thought in mind: we can examine them to see whether the changes that are wrought in them are in fact such as to suggest that the cause of the changes is what it claims to be, a raising of human life to a higher and richer level through the power of Love and Truth and Beauty.

Let us look then first at human love and marriage. And let us be clear at the outset that if religion does show us how these things can be immeasurably enriched it does so, not by weaving romantic webs of dreams in defiance of the facts, but precisely by starting from and building on the facts.

What are these facts? Long ago Aristotle defined man as a social animal. Men and women are not self-sufficient; they need society if they are to live a full, rich life economically, politically, culturally; but much deeper than that, they normally need another human being to share their life, to share the whole of it, so that they build it up—because life is something you make—together. That is what *Genesis* means when it tells us that God saw that the first man needed a helpmeet. Still more, it is what our Lord means when he talks of man and woman becoming two in one flesh. Two in one: it is just that hunger of oneness that is the stuff of love. But when you say that, you are implying three very important things, three very important facts. In the first place, you say a thing *has* pleasure or pain, but you say it *is* one: love is primarily a question not of having but of being.[1] Secondly, when you say oneness you mean total oneness, oneness on every level of life, bodily and spiritual alike. There is a sorrow which consists in the denial of bodily oneness to those whom love has made one in mind; there is also a torture which consists in conceding physical union but withdrawing the mind, withholding the deeper unity of spirit. Love wants to be wholly united with the thing it loves. And thirdly, you imply that this love-business is a long process, indeed a life-long process. Young people sometimes think that marriages are made in heaven in the sense that all they have to do is to meet someone peculiarly attractive and then marry him or her, and they will automatically live happy ever after. It is not so simple. An old English poet sang: Come, live with me and be my love; and it is indeed a question of learning, slowly, gradually, to *live* together, to build up a life together; and only in so far as that is done, through thick and thin, will the second half of the line come true and the two people concerned become fully each other's love.

[1] When you learn to love music, it becomes part of you: you *are* more than you were before. When you learn to love a human being, that love too is part of you, and you *are* more—your being is enlarged to all the extent of this new life that you are now given.

Love, then, is a necessity for the ordinary man and woman; but love means becoming something new, a change of being and of the whole of one's being; and that change takes a long time. We talk of love-*making*; and we are right; but we need to remember that there is making to be done on every level of our lives, and that it really is a making: not just the enjoyment of something given, but the gradual and sometimes painful making of what is not there to begin with.

Now one of those facts of which religion reminds us, and which otherwise might be forgotten with disastrous effects, is this: that a human being is not a body and a spirit but one single thing which is body-spirit, so that physical events affect the mind and mental events affect the body; and therefore physical love-making must be either a means to oneness of mind and heart or else exactly the opposite, a destroying of oneness of mind and heart; just as, on the other hand, a perfect unity of spirit is what brings the deepest joy to physical union. That is why, even on the physical level, the making of oneness is a long process. Sex in man is not the same as sex in animals; it is not just a little different; it is essentially different; because when a man makes love he makes love not to a body but to a human being, a body-spirit; and if it is really love that he is making, then he will regard this other human being as much more important than anything else in the world, including himself; and so he will approach his life with her with a great humility and reverence, and a great fear of hurting what he loves but what as yet he so inadequately knows. No two individuals are exactly alike in their need of expressing their love; they change moreover from moment to moment; and all this has to be learnt if love-making is not to be turned into a selfish grasping at a selfish, isolated pleasure; and it cannot be learnt in a day or a year.

There must then be a unity of minds; and it is again a hard fact of human nature that as we come to know persons more deeply we realize more and more how little we really know them. Moreover, the minds of man and woman work differently: he more rational, she more intuitive; and they have to learn to understand those differences, so as really to complement and complete each other. Young people who marry in a haze of romance and glamour sometimes think, when they have their first quarrel, that all is over; on the contrary, it should be just beginning. This unity too has to be achieved; and it cannot be achieved except through toil, and perhaps through tears.

And then beneath it all the unity of heart, of will. It is not a question of trying to eliminate every difference of taste and inclination and superficial wants; on the contrary; but there is the need of the unity of the deep personal will, because without that there can be no true sharing of life, no real making together of the home. It is this above all that you mean when you say, Come, live with me and be my love; and it is here that the process is longest.

That is why theology quarrels with some modern (and ancient) theories of love and mariage: they will not face the facts in their fullness; they will not accept the nature of things and try to act accordingly. Marriage is of its nature, and not through any man-made laws or superstitions, a life-work. Again, if you accept the facts about sex in their fullness you know that it is part of a total *human* situation; some people take what they call a purely scientific view of it, a chemical view of it, and that is not facing the facts; other people prefer to follow another poet and to gather rosebuds while they may, and they are in like case, they are using love-making for a purpose which will not produce love, for you cannot find human love by plucking in rapid succession at a variety of rosebuds—and it does not make the situation much better if the rosebuds pluck back.

No, Come *live* with me, the poet sings; and the sharing of a life includes the moments of glamour and glory but it does not mean mainly that. It consists primarily in scrubbing the house and bathing the baby. And here again the Church recalls us to reality. What it tells us is this: the poet does not say; Wait until I've bathed the baby and then come, live with me; you must not think of married life as made up of little islands of loving happiness in a vast ocean of loveless drudgery. The drudgery, the toil and no doubt the tears, you will certainly have, but if you accept them precisely as part of your making of love; if you say, I *want* to do this hard work or bear this trouble because it's for him, or for her, then you will be doing two things: you will be turning the drudgery into a labour of love and therefore into something much less like drudgery; and also you will be turning it into yet another form of love-making, you will be making it the means to a deeper understanding and love, you will be making it the stuff out of which your oneness is created. You learn to know and love men, as you learn to know and love God, not least by doing the ordinary humdrum jobs of life with them and for them.

Now among all these humdrum jobs there is one which of course takes precedence of all the rest: the making of the family. Come, *live* with me: love means, not only the hunger to be one with another human being, but also the hunger to be fulfilled by making something else in union *with* that other human being, and primarily by making a home and a family. Here again the Church recalls us to reality. There are people who want to rest in the first thing, their own love for each other; and they regard children as a nuisance, a distraction; but they are going against a very deep instinct, and they have no right to be surprised or indignant when their own unity of heart and therefore their own happiness begin to disintegrate. To turn love in upon itself, and rob it of its natural fulfilment, is to rob it of its chief creativeness and therefore to take the heart, the life, out of it.

There is an old saying, Love is self-diffusive: its whole nature is to be outward-turning, to express itself in something, as the instinct of every artist is to express the thing he sees and loves. And the Church gives us the deep religious truth behind this psychological fact when it tells us that human love is complete and perfected only when the image of the blessed Trinity is fulfilled in it: when, from the love of the two-in-one-flesh, there comes the third thing which is the expression of that love, the child. Now what we have to notice especially here is this: that while on the one hand the child is the fruit of the love and unity of the parents, on the other hand that loving unity is itself made, or made perfect, *through* the making of the family, the bearing and upbringing of the child. It is that common task, above all, that makes men and women whole; it is there that they can learn a wisdom, a patience, a common understanding and a common joy, that they could not learn elsewhere. It is that that makes them fully men and women; and that is why there is something radically wrong, terribly wrong, about a state of society in which that fundamental human right and human dignity is destroyed or even interfered with, and sooner or later such a society will pay a heavy price.

We were thinking just now of this supreme form of love-making as humdrum; and why? Because in spite of all the joy that it brings it is made up mainly of the day by day work and worry of making a home: the washing and mending, the food bills and doctor's bills and school fees, and above all the day by day struggle to build up the family into a real unity, so that the members of the family really do think, not simply in terms of their own self-centred purposes, but in terms of their common life and love. And why should they, people sometimes argue? Why this erection of the family into an ideal when what really matters is simply the individual boy or girl? And once again the Church is on the side of the realities of life: we need only think for a moment of the typical spoilt child, selfish, undisciplined and therefore unendurable, to see at once how it is precisely because it is the individual boy or girl that matters that the family is a necessity.

But still, when you have the work of building up the family happily done, still the making of love is not complete, for still love is outward-turning; and as the unit is now the family, so, to express its common love, it turns outward again to the world about it and finds there the material it needs. Most of us must have known at some time the misery of going to the sort of home which is in reality only a house that happens to be shared by a number of individuals with the same name; there is something dead about it because it can make nothing, for indeed there is no *it*. But we know too those other homes which are homes indeed: the homes where there is always a welcome and words that are kind, the homes you go to instinctively when you are in trouble, sure that they will make things better—because making, renewing life, renewing hope, renewing joy in the world, is what they automatically do. It is there, in those homes, that you find human life at last in its fullness. A man is more than a body and spirit; he extends his personality in the work of his hands and his brain, the things he uses, the plot of earth that is his, the people he shares his life with; and so it is here that you find the fullness of life because it is here that the personality is fully engaged, radiating outwards the life of love, first to the one, and then to the many who make up the family, and thence, with them, to the greater family which is the world.

This is life in its natural fullness. But the Church can do more than recall us to some of the natural facts we tend to lose sight of: it has a greater message than that. To that message we must now come. But first let us note this: that all that we have seen so far stresses the fact that love is hard. The Bible tells us, love is strong as death, and many waters shall not quench it. And indeed it needs to be so if it is to take all this troublesome and sometimes rebellious material and turn it into joy and happiness and peace. There is a time, when love is young, when what would be drudgery is itself a joy and therefore easy; but then there comes the time when that first fine frenzy fades and the hardness begins. It is a time, not indeed to throw up the hands and cry that all is over, but to roll up the sleeves and say that all is beginning; for this is where the making of the real, deep love and understanding is to be done.

But it must inevitably be hard, because the hardest thing in the world for man, since the fall of man, is to stop being self-centred. When a young man is vouchsafed his own particular vision, the one human being who is like no other human being, then a revolution takes place within him: he finds that the centre of his life is no longer his own ego but this intruder from without. That is the definition of love: the making of the centre of life not the self but the other. And as long as the first glamorous thrill continues, his new condition presents itself to him not as a problem or a purgatory but as a glory. But that period is given precisely in order that in it he may learn gradually but easily how to deepen his new life which is so much at variance with his self-regarding instincts, so that his love may become deep and true and unshakeable. That work remains to be done: the work of making his self-dedication not an affair of the superficial emotions merely but of his deepest will; and once again it is a work that takes a lifetime to achieve. And so it is partly *because* of this hardness, *because* of the demands love puts on human nature, and the terrible ease with which this adventure can end in failure, that marriage is made a sacrament for us, a means whereby we can call on the power and the energizing life of God himself.

It is as well to say life rather than use the theological term grace, for the word grace tends to become a familiar label the real meaning of which we forget. We need to think, for instance, of that first Whitsunday, when the apostles were huddled together in an upstairs room, hiding behind barred doors for fear of the Jews, and the Spirit of God came upon them—and the symbol is that of a mighty wind, rushing through the room, filling the room with its tempestuous energy—and immediately they burst through the doors and out into the street, their fears forgotten, fearing neither pain nor death, and they cried aloud to the world the wonderful works of God. That sort of power, that sort of energy, that renewal of life which was then bestowed upon them, vivid as tongues of flame, that infusion of a life far greater than that of man, is what we mean by the grace of the sacraments. It is not magic: the power is offered but it needs to be used, it needs every effort on our part; but it is a power which in this case can make light of the difficulties and turn them into triumphs of love, and turn love itself from the niggardly timorous self-regarding little emotion that it might have been into a mighty fire that at the end can enkindle the heart of the world.

But christian marriage is more than that. The Church starts from the assumption that men and women want to be happy, and have a right to want to be happy; and therefore all that is presupposed and included. But what is it, in the last resort, that makes us happy and that alone can make us fully happy? We come back to the words of Augustine: Thou hast made us for thyself, and our heart can find no rest until it rest in thee. The ideal of christian marriage is not something less than that of other marriages: it is infinitely more. We are here only finding a particular application for what we saw before as a general principle: all the human things that go to make up the fullness of man's destiny, all the things that make him man the lover and man the maker: they all find their fullness only in so far as they are caught up into the infinity of the life of God. The substance of our destiny is that we are called to share in the infinite happiness of God. So it is with love and marriage. John loves his Susan, and with his Susan he is happy; but if they are to be perfectly happy, if they are to reach the fullness of stature of redeemed humanity, then they must come hand in hand, joint makers of their life and love and home, to offer *him* what they have made and are making, and to enrich their love for each other by making it a part of their love for him.

To *enrich* their love: the first duty of God's human creatures is to sing to God: to sing in their life and love and work as well as their words, to make all that they do an act of praise; but in doing that they find their finite life taking on the richness of infinity. When John first falls in love with Susan he finds that his other interests are not deadened but on the contrary given new life: the grass is greener, the sky a richer blue, music has more to say to him, his work takes on a new interest. It is the same with the soul's discovery of God. That is the supreme thought

A.H.

in the christian theology of marriage: this, the Church tells us, is the christian's normal way of coming to know and love and serve God and so to be happy, happy with all the happiness of God; and because for this adventure above all you need the mighty power of infinite life, that power is given in the sacrament.

But it is John and Susan themselves who are the ministers of this sacrament; it is they who give God's life to each other; it is they who are to lead each other, and who together are to lead their children, to the heart of God which is their ultimate resting-place, their ultimate home. When Dante gazes into the eyes of Beatrice in Paradise he sees in them not his own image but the figure of Christ to whom she is to lead him: it is the symbol of all real christian love. The lover is ultimately and completely fulfilled, as a lover, only when his human love is caught up into the splendour of the infinite consuming Fire, so that in his revealing of his human love to the human being whom he loves it is God himself who is revealed. Come, live with me, the poet sings; but it is for the christian to sing, Come, live with me in the heart of God: there we shall find, there we shall know, what love really is, what the fullness, the glory, the thrill of life can really be.

We live in sad and troubled days. We have seen the war and its misery, and now the war is over, but not the misery. Wherever you look in the world there seem to be greed and selfishness and fear and cruelty, and the hatred to which these things give rise. And these things go very deep: it is the very nature of man that is threatened with destruction. As the Russian thinker Berdyaev has put it, we are witnessing not, as so often in the past, a crisis in human history, but the crisis of human history. The world refused the divine destiny that was offered it; and now we realize all too clearly that in doing so it was also inevitably attacking humanity itself. Today, in economics, in politics, in social life, it is human nature itself that is being *destroyed*. We stand on the edge of the abyss. But there is one thing, and one thing only, that is stronger than hatred of God and humanity, and it is love of God and humanity.

That is why there is one thing we must never allow ourselves to do: we must never think, Of course I hate this misery and injustice and hatred and fear and I want men and women to be happy—but what can I do about it? Perhaps the ordinary men and women, the common folk, can do more about it than many a famous politician. The world is in danger of death because it lacks the understanding, and the reality, of love. But it is just that that they can give it. They can make their own lives, their own homes, a living expression of love; they can show forth, by what they are, to those who come in contact with them, the living might and the mighty pity of the God who is love; and if they do that, then that love and pity will inevitably go out from them to heal others and to uphold other homes in the likeness of their own; and then these others in their turn will pass on that spirit of love and gentleness and peace; and so, in the end, through them and others like them, the world may be healed and comforted and renewed.

Chapter 10: WHAT IS EDUCATION?

In the beginning God planted a garden; and he gave it to the man he had formed, to dress it and keep it. And he walked with Adam in the garden in the cool of the evening.

All living is meant to be making for God and with God: we are still meant to be God's gardeners, even though the garden is choked with thorns and thistles and to keep it we have to toil and sweat. But God is gracious; we do not toil and sweat in loneliness. He made for Adam a helpmeet, that they might be two in one, and, being makers together, might be fulfilled in the three-in-one, the human image of the Trinity, the family. To make this unity, and then in the warmth and light of this unity to dress and keep God's garden, to make with one's hands or head and to make for God and with God: this is the destiny of the sons and daughters of Adam. But before making these things, and in making them, we must make ourselves; for we come forth from God trailing clouds of glory indeed but weak and helpless and unformed, in no condition to be creators until we have grown in body and mind and heart. We need education. It begins in the cradle; it ends, if we are wise, only in the tomb. If we are clear about what we ought to be, we shall be clear about what education ought to be: that process of growth which turns us into creators, creators of ourselves, our families, our world, our worship.

To create we must first love; to love we must first know. Life is discovery; but discovery, not with the mind in isolation, but with body, mind and heart. The personality must either grow as a unity, or decay. Education is either the education of the personality as a whole, or it is not education at all. To know, to love, to serve: these things are not growth to fullness but disruption unless they are the knowledge and love and service of the One, and of the many in the One.

Omnia in ipso—all things are yours and you are Christ's and Christ is God's. We cannot be creators unless we know and love the world about us; but we cannot be fully creators unless we see the world in God and God in the world. One of the darkest of educational heresies is that which supposes that education means simply the

imparting of information. There are two kinds of knowledge: knowledge about things and knowledge of things
—information and vision. As faith, which is knowledge
about God, is fulfilled in vision of God, so the information which is knowledge about the world is fulfilled in
awareness and vision of the world. We need information
in order to create; but we shall never create, however well-
informed we are, unless we see. Nor shall we create unless
we love; but it is seeing that begets love. As faith directs all
our knowledge, our information, in order that all our
knowledge may be one, so too that sense of God which is
our nearest approach on earth to vision must direct all our
seeing, that all our seeing may be one. The first essential
purpose of education therefore is to make us see: to make
us see God and the world, and God in the world; so that
seeing we may love, and loving we may worship, and
worshipping we may create.

The imparting of information is, in the last resort, a
means to that end. It is useful to know as many as possible
of the facts of history; but not simply and solely as an
assemblage of facts. Knowledge of the past needs to be
brought to life, to become a real living awareness of the
past, a living sense of tradition for instance, or a living
sympathy with, and therefore a vital assimilation of, the
idiom of a past culture; and then this knowledge of fact
can find a further fulfilment in wise judgement—only so
can you be a historian instead of a dictionary of facts and
dates—and so, finally, can help our awareness and judgement of the present, and our power of creation for the
future. All studies can thus be directed to awareness and
creation: mathematics can give a sense of order and structure; history can help us to struggle with the problems of
today, learning from the mistakes as well as from the accu-
mulated wisdom of the past; geography shows us what our

brother-men are doing in the world, what they are like, how they are serving humanity or need the help of humanity, so that we may help humanity the better in our turn.

And apart from all these and kindred sciences there is the study of art and poetry—in prose and verse—for this means essentially, not the imparting of information at all, but the learning of immediate awareness and vision: not acquaintance with a vast number of historical facts, data, textual problems, or a familiarity with the private lives of authors, but an immediate awareness of the poet's experience, an immediate awareness of the reality expressed, an immediate oneness too, where the past is concerned, with a living tradition, so as to ensure that we shall be creators in our turn because we shall have the stuff of poetry in us.

Information is indeed, in this setting, an essential part of education. But even so it will be dangerous unless we develop the faculty of judgement and criticism; reading is dangerous without discrimination. The power of the press, and of propanganda generally, is too obvious to need emphasis. If the news is interesting, as a boy once said, the papers sell like wild flowers. We need training in criticism.

This is true even—or rather, primarily—in the context of religious education. It is a very short-sighted policy to bring up children in a hothouse atmosphere from which all adverse criticism of their faith and morality is excluded, so that when they leave school the unchristian or antichristian influences about them will find them unprepared and unarmed to meet them. They may well be bowled over by this new, sudden, unsuspected world unless they have been trained to think about it for themselves beforehand. We need to be critical; and we shall not criticize adequately unless all our criticism, of art, of literature, of history, of life in our own day, springs from a single source, a God-given knowledge of God which itself has been deeply considered and assimilated and made our own. A catholic history is not one which insists that all catholics have been white as snow and all non-catholics black as ink: that is neither history nor catholicism; it is simply one that sees all history, the past and the future together, the good and the evil together, in the light of the supreme historical event, the Incarnation of the Word of God. So too the study of religion is not the study of religious truths *in vacuo,* but an attempt to understand them in relation to everyday life and secular knowledge and awareness, that through this supreme study all studies may be unified.

And here above all, information is not enough; here above all the aim is not to know all the answers parrot-wise—answers that will dissolve into thin air at the first approach of opposition or argument. It is, first, to assimilate the truth: by a rational, critical approach, a proper weighing of the problems, a real attempt to think about them for oneself. It is secondly, therefore, to be really able to judge: to see the reasons for things—for the moral law, for instance—and therefore to be able to judge the events or the views of everyday in the light of principles which are securely held because they are really personal, really assimilated. But to be able to judge for oneself with humility: to be wise enough to be able to say, Yes, I have been taught to think for myself but I have not been taught everything: there are many things I cannot expect to understand all at once, and therefore I cannot expect my own judgement to be adequate, I cannot expect to be in possession of all the facts, all the aspects of the problems; and so I shall still listen to others, I shall still treat my own ability to judge reality with a certain definite reserve. And then finally, and above all, the aim is to make these rational studies the servant of the faculty of vision, to have rehearsed them walking with God, to have turned them—and with them all the knowledge and awareness they direct—from the water of science into the wine of supernatural life and love.

The mind is dependent on the body. We hurt the mind if we either neglect the body or attend to its development as though it were an independent entity. Education is the education of the whole personality. We are dependent on our senses—on the acuteness and delicacy and accuracy of our sense-perceptions—for our awareness of the world about us; we are largely dependent on the well-being of the body for the right balance of the mind. The criterion is again the demands of personal vision and power of creation in oneness with God: sport, for example, is good for the body, but if it is turned into a fetish it is bad for the personality; if it is so highly organized as to exclude private initiative and creation it is bad for the personality; if it is brutalizing it is bad, however beneficial it may be on the purely physical level; if it develops community awareness and community spirit it is good, if it merely plays down to the herd instinct it is bad.

We belong not to a herd but to a family: a family of persons, independent, creative, capable of judgement and initiative, yet all creating together as a unity because all together finding material for creation in the stuff of the common life and in the service of the common life. To that point we must return in a moment; what is immediately relevant here is the place of the emotional life in education as a whole. It might be said that education is successful in so far as it substitutes love for fear as the motive of work. Information can be imparted at the end of a stick; awareness cannot. The love motive means, first and foremost, love of the reality of which the pupil is made aware; and indeed that love can be aroused as a rule only in so far as the reality is presented not as abstract proposition but as living reality and material of creation.

But the relationship between pupil and teacher, and between the pupils themselves, must also be of great importance.[1] In the former case there must at least be an atmosphere of emotional harmony and sympathy. Education has its inescapable drudgery, like every other aspect of human life; but in that atmosphere it is possible, given imagination and an ability to make people laugh, to turn even the drudgery into something interesting—though one imagines that few who have tried it would describe it as easy.

Between the pupils themselves, the spirit of rivalry which so aptly prepares them to acquiesce in a world of cut-throat competition needs to be replaced as far as possible by a spirit of concreation, the idea that all are making something together, are contributing to a common work.

All this is an ideal; in practice, as Plato said, the boy must be bound by many bridles; we shall turn children into spineless hedonists if we abolish discipline; but it is an ideal that can be approached, and that can determine the sort of compromise that fallen nature makes necessary. And that at least it must do; because otherwise we are not educating, we are merely making a child learn facts by rote. Knowledge, as the life of the spirit, is only fulfilled in love; but love follows, not from an abstract knowledge of propositions, but from direct awareness of reality. The

[1] The mind and personality cannot grow in an atmosphere of emotional repression. The prudery which attempts to suppress the emotional life of the child through its natural stages of development, the obscurantism which attempts to arrest that development by a foolish censorship, by the cult of ignorance, and so on, are bound to have disastrous and lasting effects: are bound, among other things, to arrest mental development, and the development of character too.

genesis of the art-work is in three moments: to see, to fall
in love, and to express, first in the mind and then with the
hands; and as all living is making, so the life-process itself
is expressible in terms of those three moments. The only
adequate education is that which presents all reality to be
seen, and loved, in God, that there may follow from this
vision the will to create for God.

The primary form of creation for most men and women
is procreation, the making of the family. Mention of discipline may bring us back to the ideal of the family, for
discipline too can be presented and ought to be presented
creatively; and it is most easily and valuably done in terms
of family life. *Vae nostris natibus,* Erasmus is reputed to
have said of his school days; and he was expressing the
common experience of many long centuries of suffering
youth. Today it is better realized that discipline both inside
and outside the classroom can be something which the
young can rationally and critically accept and creatively
establish.[1] Little boys tend to regard the *fiat* of a head-
master as something binding but arbitrary and inscrutable
like the *fiat* of a fickle deity; but a school as a whole can be
induced to see the necessity of regulation in general as the
condition of an orderly and happy family life, and can to
some extent be invited to share in the creation of that order
by discussion of particular rulings.

So the young can learn to obey; for obedience is the act
of a free man, not of an automaton; an act of choice, not a
submission to superior force or to fear. As they grow older
they may take a responsible part in government; and so

---

[1] A slap is still good medicine for hysteria; and similarly there are still
times when the normal healthy child does need some sort of physical
correction as a kind of shock therapy to restore equilibrium. To abolish
discipline altogether is not to train the child to creation but to abandon it
to disintegration.

they learn to be citizens, whose office it is not blindly to follow a leader but creatively to preserve—or if necessary to help to change—the order of society. But so also they learn the yet more important lesson of family life, if the school is run on family lines, the rather cold, rational co-operation of the city-state replaced by the more intimate and informal atmosphere of home and all discipline tempered by humour and motived by love.

For it is the family, not the State, that the school community ought to resemble. First of all because school life is defensible at all only in so far as it is a prolongation of family life—for to send a child into an atmosphere of cold impersonal efficiency, where order is kept and results are obtained by an equally cold and impersonal use of sanctions, is as good for the child as to put it out to nurse with a nest of scorpions.

But the catholic school must resemble the family also because it must be a part of the life of the Church, which is not a State but a family. The Church is the communion of saints and the communion of sinners; we are each responsible for all: and together we are meant to build up the life of the Church, to carry on the work of the development of dogma, to share in that common priesthood of the laity which gives them a part in the redemptive activity of Christ in the world. But to do that we must love the world with something of the love with which God so loved the world; and to do that we must see. We must each give our own special offering to the world; and to do that we must have creative initiative. We must be able to discern the true and the good and the beautiful from the false and the sham; and to do that we must have judgement. We must also—and this is the most important of all —we must also have humility, to serve the world in God's way and not in ours; and to do that we must have learnt docility, the essential complement, in all activity, to initiative. There is no great art without reverence.

Those schools which are run on the assumption that the child can do no wrong and must therefore be allowed always to do whatever it likes are, among other things, teaching the child pride instead of humility, and so preventing it from ever being a creator of good things. On the other hand those schools which set out to prevent the child from thinking for itself, destroying its power of initiative and killing its spirit, teaching it not to reason why—teaching it indeed that there is no reason why there should be a reason why—these are teaching not humility but subhumanity. Humility does mean respect for the teacher, the respect given by one free human being to another; but primarily it means respect for reality: the attitude of mind that worships truth as something infinitely greater than itself, something that may with God's grace take possession of it, not something that can be seized and turned into a cash proposition.

And how is this lesson to be learnt? Only by learning to see and to love. *Scientia inflat*: the man who knows a great deal about things but has never learnt to see, tends to be assertive; the man who has once lost his heart to a blade of grass or a glow-worm and sensed God's omnipresence within them is at least on the road to reverence.

Education concerns body, mind, and will, not in isolation but in unity, because its aim is the growth of the personality. The body ministers to the mind in the business of seeing and loving reality, and again in the work of making reality. The mind needs information, needs growth in knowledge; but still more it needs vision, the growth of awareness, and discrimination, the growth of judgement; above all, it needs the vision of unity, the knowledge and love of all things in the knowledge and love of the One;

only from all these is wisdom born. The mind is incomplete without the heart; the emotions are part of the integral life of man and must play their part in education, not simply in the sense that a proper outlet must be found for them, but in the sense that they too minister to the birth and growth of wisdom. The will has to be trained to obey and to rule; to be humble and creative; to serve the family and to act with independent initiative; and all this too is part of wisdom. And all these elements in the complete man go to form the creative man; the man who creates in himself, in his family, in his work, in his worship, in the life of the Church. When the child, the youth, the man, has learnt and is learning these things, he has learnt and is learning to know and love and serve God, and that is the end of education; for so he will, whatever his troubles and sufferings, be happy with him even in this world, and perfectly, in the cool of the eternal evening, in the next.

Chapter 11: ART AND EDUCATION

If now we go on to consider the question of education and art, the first thing that must strike us in the light of what has already been said is this: that while we can hardly over-estimate the importance of education in art, we may falsify the issue badly if we speak of art in education. The purpose of education, we have seen, is not primarily to impart information; it is not simply to give enough instruction to enable the pupils later on to be misled by the newspapers or to make them efficient technical operatives. It must include the formation of a critical mind. But as we also saw, man is a many-levelled being; and education must be concerned with all those levels, not in isolation from one another as though they were separate entities but as elements in a unity: a healthy and well-built body, an alert and critical mind, a will trained to love and strive after the true, the good and the beautiful, all together making up the fullness of the unified body-spirit. And we learn to know and love and grow to our full spiritual stature through the senses.

If education is simply divided up into so many hours for the training of the body, so many hours for the pursuit of knowledge, animal fitness regarded as one isolated objective, the passing of examinations another, then it is failing in its object: first, because the result will be not the unity but the disruption of the personality, and secondly because it is neglecting the primary purpose of teaching, the growth in awareness. Wordsworth's account of the fading of the visionary gleam, the dispelling of the clouds of glory, the burial of intuition beneath the shades of the rational and utilitarian prison-house, is a radical criticism of education as too many have known it. In the Middle Ages they put the accent, in the *trivium,* on reason and science; but they could afford to, for the environment was such as to keep the perceptive and affective, the intuitive and aesthetic elements in the personality thoroughly alive. Today it is otherwise. And if those who have charge of education think of it in terms of an intensive pumping of information into the young brain, with intervals for physical training, they are doing their best to perpetuate the horrors of a civilization of artless industry and uncreative life.

But again, suppose an education which does produce a young man or woman deeply aware and appreciative of the world of created things, well read and informed, keenly critical, vitally grafted into a living tradition, and experiencing, judging and acting as a unity, an integral personality: there would still be two things lacking. You cannot make a personality which is complete and rounded off in itself, like an art-work. Man is only complete, in the first place, when he is making something other than himself; all living is making; and the aim of education therefore is to produce makers, to produce men and women who will think of life as a whole, of all life personal and social alike, as something to be created by their efforts. To speak of art *in* education is thus liable to be disastrous because the whole of education ought in a sense to be an education in art.

The second element which would still be lacking is one at which we glanced in the last chapter: the counterpart and pre-condition of creativity: the sense of reverence. The Renaissance attempted to construct a civilization, a creative humanism, whose centre and criterion should be man. We are reaping now what was then sown. We alone of all historical civilizations have come to think of reality as something to be seized upon by the mind, taken possession of, and then bent to our own uses. Our attitude is not that of Milton's nun, her rapt soul sitting in her eyes, but of a captain of industry. Augustine was wiser when in one of his letters he described the way to wisdom as: firstly humility and secondly humility and thirdly humility.

The history of post-Renaissance Europe follows a logical course. In spite of material and technical progress it is the history, as we now at last have been forced to see, of a gradual diminution in the stature of man. Wordsworth's Ode finds here a social application. The Renaissance world of man-centred humanism, from which infinity had been excluded, dwindled into the world of rationalism, the Age of Enlightenment, from which all the deeper and richer awareness within human experience was excluded in its turn; and this finally made way for the age of scientific materialism in which man became simply economic man, the servant of subhuman forces beyond his control. It was only to be expected that the spirit of man, thus degraded and neglected, should take its revenge. We cannot live by science alone; we cannot live by reason alone; and the instinctive, intuitive and religious elements in human nature re-asserted themselves.

The re-assertion, because it was disruptive rather than re-creative, was often disastrous. Too often it made two fatal mistakes. It went to the opposite extreme and rejected the rational altogether; it also confused the supra-rational with the sub-rational. We have seen the process at work in the realms of art, of politics, of religion. To abolish reason is to reduce human life to a formless chaos. But it is not enough to distinguish the rational from the non-rational. The process whereby at the pre-conscious and instinctive level we react to an object of fear or desire is specifically different from the process at the conscious and intuitive level whereby we see and become one with the beauty of a tree, a pot, a symphony. The former process is sub-rational, the latter supra-rational; and the three things, the rational, the sub-rational, and the supra-rational, are not further reducible. All are essential elements in complete humanity; and we shall never restore the diminished stature of man by reasserting one element while ignoring the others.

If we are witnessing or about to witness the end of economic man—and one can only hope devoutly that we are—then we must choose. If our history in recent centuries proves anything at all, it surely proves that man cannot be just human. Alone of all historical civilizations we tried to renounce contemplation, worship, mysticism; we called them mistiness and mirage and turned them out; and now we have seen them return, by the back door. Art suffered like everything else. There is something sadly hollow about the grandiosities of an art whose aim is purely to extol the human. Subtly you find it, as Eric Gill pointed out, in a place like the Piazza of St. Peter's; blatantly in such erections as the Vittorio Emmanuele monument in the same city. There is no great art without reverence; and reverence for what is human, necessary though it is, is not of itself sufficient: it tends to forget its humour and become ludicrous, or pathetic. The only antidote to that—the only real and radical return to sanity—is the making of holy pictures: and any good picture is holy in so far as it proceeds from reverence and is therefore an act of worship —the subject-matter is irrelevant. It is right and proper to reverence created things; it is indeed a lesson that our world has to re-learn; but that reverence is robbed of its depth and its unity and its completion if it is not integrated in the worship of the One. The love of Nature, apart from man, tends to become a selfish and irresponsible aestheticism; the love of man, apart from God, tends to become a snobbish and socially irresponsible worship of an ideal projection, quite compatible with hatred and contempt of men and women. Hume affirmed that universal love of humanity is an impossibility; and naturally speaking no doubt he was right.

The last element, then, and the most important, in the personality whose growth education has to foster, is the element of reverence, of creatureliness, of contemplation. It is the counterpart and pre-condition of creation because creation, if it is to be worth while, must be the expression of contemplation. The vulgarities of our posters and picture-magazines are sufficiently obvious examples of what happens when contemplation is replaced, as motive of making, by commerce.

If all this is valid; if the principal aim of education is to produce contemplative creators; then the importance of

A.H.

the art-teacher at the present time can hardly be over-stressed. It would be disastrous to speak of art in education if by that were implied the theory that art, the making of things, were simply one of many departments in education. Art, like religion in this, is not ultimately a department in education but is co-terminous with education. The study of painting and carving and so on can both stimulate and be stimulated by the study of other things. If the child is himself making pots and pans and pictures he will be interested to see the sort of pots and pans and pictures which they made in ancient Egypt or Greece or Rome; and equally his acquaintance with those survivals of the past will stimulate his imagination and creativity in the present. But the thing is far deeper and wider than that. The chief importance of the study of the arts is that it stimulates creativity generally; and therefore tends to make the child, and youth, and man, think creatively about life in general.

The art-teacher can thus be chiefly responsible for an attitude of mind which is invaluable in all other studies. At the same time those other studies in their turn must, if they are not to bring down the shades of the prison-house upon the growing boy, be primarily a matter of an ever-deepening awareness, and an invitation to that creation which is the natural sequel to aesthetic and intuitive discovery. What a monstrous travesty of education it is to fill the heads of boys and girls with details of the dates and sources and textual divergences of Shakespeare's plays instead of helping them to see them for what they are, a revelation of the beauty and tragedy and meaning of life, an open door not merely to thought about life but to life itself. The intuitive powers of the child are keen and deep: it is we who stifle them. We turn the real world, the world which is his birthright, the world of being, into a collection of lifeless labels; we teach him to know about it, but in the process we kill in him what would make him fully a man, we kill the contemplative and the creator.

But there is a further danger, which may assail precisely those who are concerned to rescue the young from becoming simply passive recipients of information—and later, passive-minded automata at work, passive recipients in leisure—the danger of activism. We do not make creators of the young simply by seeing to it that they are always at something, always active and busy and handy. It is the same in the social sphere. There is urgent need for action; that can hardly be in dispute. But it will be the wrong sort of action if it is not the overflow of contemplation. Right doing follows upon right being. Our first duty therefore, once again, is to make contemplatives: to help the young to see the real world, to see the real world in itself, which means to see the world in God and God in the world. Then, if we can stimulate their creativity, we are by that very fact teaching them implicitly to criticize the evils of our man-made system, but to criticize it, not with the detached abstract criticism of the academic but with the vital, painful, creative criticism of the man who knows that he is criticizing his own world, himself. Then indeed a desire for creation in this sphere also is born; and this is the time for explicit study of sociological problems, and then there follows the time for action. To attempt to make a short cut through that process is surely fatal; and will lead to the formation only of the doctrinaire, of the man who knows the text-book answers and is certainly not lacking in zeal, but who rides roughshod over the things he should most reverence and defend, the dignity and beauty of the world in general and of the human personality in particular.

It is not, of course, that we should be saints before we

enter the world of action—if that were so nothing would be done. But what is essential is that we should enter the world of action with a right orientation of our being, in radical oneness with being. That is the essential work of education; and that is why all education is in a real sense an education in art. That is why also, at the present moment, when education is still so largely held in the grip of a false theory, the new world of art teaching must be called in to redress the balance of the old.

We are still forced very largely to do the bulk of our real educational work outside the educational curriculum; the study of painting and poetry and the rest can act as the thin end of the wedge, inserting itself triumphantly into the curriculum itself. It is not only that these things can provide a necessary psychological outlet and mode of expression for children who otherwise would be inhibited at school; it is not only that these things supply an element in human growth without which the personality is stunted; it is primarily that these things can safeguard and stimulate the awareness and contemplative reverence and creativity without which study must remain bookish, impersonal and dead.

But all this is so only if the teaching of art is made quite definitely, not an elegant and more or less esoteric parasite on the existing social structure, but a protest against it: if it is made quite clear that art is not a matter of the occasional occupation of leisure but the everyday vocation of everyman; that there is no specific difference between the making of pictures and poems and the making of pots and carts and gardens and ships and cities and states and unions of states; and that a world in which the work of everyday is not creation and vocation is a world that is doomed. Most discussions lead back to education as they lead back to theology; we can only make a better world by making a demand for a better world; and we can only create that demand through education. The art teachers of today are thus revealed as the midwives of the world of tomorrow.

The word vocation has just introduced itself; and it is with that idea that we must complete these reflections. We have been living in an atmosphere of inherited individualism from which only a crisis can shake us; and the idea of life and work as not merely a means to personal security or enrichment but a social function carried out within the unity of worship is one that is not easy to instil. Here again the influence which art can exert is enormous. It can exert a direct influence inasmuch as the individual concrete thing appeals to the young mind where the abstract and general baffles it; and the idea of making for others is easier to instil than the idea of doing for others. It can influence indirectly inasmuch as it can open the mind to beauties which of themselves and perhaps unconsciously drive home the lesson that man is a social animal: the social commentaries, the satires, the deep human insights into human community, of poets and dramatists and sculptors and novelists. It was wisely said that the business of poetry is not to save the soul but to make the soul worth saving; and the same applies to all art. Only when that business is doing is there the possibility, the material, of a better world. The present situation might well seem very like a vicious circle: we must look not least to the art teachers to break the circle and to let us out.

Chapter 12: PRAYER AND POLITICS (I)

We have been considering the implications of the picture of man in relation to some of the elements in his personal life as lover and maker. We have seen the essential importance of the faculty of vision if that life is to be full and complete: vision of the world of created things as a unity, unified in the omnipresence of God; and vision, above all, of God himself, in whose infinite life the personality at last fulfils its destiny. It remains for us to see those same implications in the wider context of man's political life, his relation to the world.

Nobody is likely nowadays to think that all is right with the world; we are much more likely to think that all is wrong with the world. But what, in the last resort, is the reason for all our troubles? There is one answer which ought to be considered; an answer for which the preceding pages have prepared us. And it is an answer which is given by others besides the christian thinkers and writers. You find it, for instance, in two recent books of Mr Aldous Huxley, *Grey Eminence* and *The Perennial Philosophy*.[1] In the former he quotes the words, Where there is no vision the people perish; and in both he argues that a world without prayer would be a world totally blind and insane; and that if, as is the case, we ourselves are dangerously far advanced into the darkness it is precisely because our world has ceased to be contemplative, has forgotten how to pray.

Now the first thing to notice about this view of the essential importance of prayer is that it is not an odd or uncommon view. It is not only Mr Huxley's view: it is the christian view; it is also the view of all the great religious teachers of the world; and more than that, it is a view which all the civilizations of the world throughout its history have held and on which they have based their life—with the one single exception of our own. If then we imagine ourselves as having to give an account of our society to the rest of humanity, we might imagine our

[1] Cf. *Appendix* A, below.

judges saying to us: Yes, you have done mighty things and good things; you have mastered Nature; you have gained wealth and power; you can live in great comfort and travel at immense speed; your science has given great gifts to humanity. But you have forgotten the one thing necessary: you have forgotten that being is more important than doing. What is the use of being able to travel at breathless speed if you have no idea where, ultimately, you want to go, or why? What is the good of conquering the air if you cannot use your conquest for the good of humanity rather than its harm? Science can tell you how to do things: it cannot tell you what you ought to do, still less what you ought to be. You have gained enormously in knowledge, and therefore in power; but you have lost your vision; and where there is no vision the people perish.

Now if this is true, if we have indeed lost the one thing that matters most, the thing on which everything else depends, if it is true that already we are dangerously far advanced into the darkness, dangerously near total blindness and insanity: then clearly we must do something to remedy the situation, and do it quickly. There is no time to lose.

Let us then think once again: what is this prayer? Why is it regarded as of such immense importance by everybody except ourselves? And what has it to do with our workaday world? What do we mean by prayer?

We have been thinking of the difference between knowing things and merely knowing about things. We may learn a great deal about some very lovely and loveable personality; but that does not enable us to say that we know him; on the contrary, we say we want to know him. And if we do come to know him intimately, and love him, then we acquire a new kind of knowledge, the knowledge that begets love and is in turn begotten by love. This is the deepest and most exciting kind of knowledge because it enlarges not our minds only but our whole personality. And what is true of persons is true also of things —of Nature, of animals, flowers, trees: it is one thing to know about them and quite another to have seen them, gazed at them, and loved them. This direct love-knowledge is what we mean by vision.

A false system of education can deaden this power of vision within us, as we have seen; the struggle for existence in our industrialized world, where we have to use things and even persons simply as means for the doing of a job, can complete the process of destruction. But poets, artists, saints, all in different ways do keep their power of seeing things as they really are; and so they are always falling in love with things, and life for them is a constant delight even though they have many sorrows to bear. Children have this power in their own simple and vivid way; and we have to learn from them: Unless ye become as little children ye shall not enter the kingdom. We have to learn how to grow out of our childishness and to become childlike: to be re-born with the heart of a child.

Now there is one thing we notice especially about little children as about saints: all the things that come their way they treat as equally real, equally part of the great family of creation. You find them having long talks with puppies, flowers, dolls, human beings, all with equal gravity. They are much wiser than we. Even though we look long and lovingly at things we shall lose our power of vision and perish unless we see them all, together, as a family in God and see God in them. Things will not yield up their deepest reality to us unless we do this; without this sense of God we touch only the fringe of reality, and even that we may easily spoil. The love of Nature may make us selfish and shallow unless it is set in the love of humanity;

we may love humanity, but that will not prevent us from being cruel to men and women unless our love for humanity is set in the love of God. Is not man's heart an abyss, asked Augustine, a deep so profound as to be hidden even from him in whom it is? Religion answers, yes; and teaches that only by the Infinite can the abyss be filled, so that we must be ready to sacrifice everything if need be for this one thing necessary, this pearl of great price, the vision of God. Only when we have found God, say the men of prayer, will our humanity be fulfilled; and only then will our eyes be fully opened to the things of this world; only then shall we be able to love them fully and without fear of turning their gold into the dross of self-love and self-glory; only then, loving humanity truly, shall we be in a position to attempt the building of a world fit for humanity.

We should not of course seek God in order to build a good and happy world: that would be the exact reverse of the true scale of values, the exact opposite of what we are here for. But we cannot as a matter of fact expect to build a good world unless we do in the first place seek God. Political changes cannot help us, Mr Huxley insists, unless many people set out to change themselves, and to change themselves by the only known method which really works, the method of the men of prayer. As long as there is no vision the people will perish. The longer we remain content with our loss of vision the further we advance into the darkness, the nearer we approach to total blindness and insanity.

Does all this seem very remote from what we usually mean by prayer? Some people think of prayer as just a way of guarding against the possible anger of God: if that is our idea of it it is a very crude one. Others think of it simply as a means to obtaining what they want: and that is not very noble either, if that is all; it is like marrying God for his money. We must indeed stand in awe of God and in fear of sin: the vastness of the universe is his footstool and his love is a burning and consuming fire. We have to ask for what we need, for we deny our nature if we refuse to admit that we are his creatures, dependent on him as children are dependent on their parents. But prayer is ultimately not so much an action as a state of being: from our point of view we should ask first of all not what it does for us but what it does to us. The wise men of the world tell us, not so much that without prayer we shall fail to get what we want, or get what we do not want, but that without prayer we shall fail to be what we want to be, we shall fail to be real men. Prayer is the vision of God, in so far as we on earth can speak of vision. Without it we shall be blind and insane. We shall only be half, or less than half, alive.

I am come, said our Lord, that they may have life. Again and again in the Gospel we find this offering of life. The world had lost its power of vision, its power to walk with God in the cool of the evening, and was perishing; but in him was life, and the life was the light of men; the darkness—that darkness into which we are so far advanced—did not comprehend it, and still does not comprehend it; but still the light is there, shining, if we have eyes to see.

The Gospel tells us of two men who said to him, Master, where dwellest thou? And he answered, Come and see. And they came, and saw where he abode, and they tarried with him. To a sad and troubled world, a world which asks despairingly, Where is peace? where is truth? where are justice and love and brotherhood? God still replies simply, Come and see. But he does not coerce his free creatures: he calls to them. He does not destroy the nature of his handiwork; it is left to us to do that. If we want to see we must make the journey.

It is a frightening thing perhaps, this pilgrim's progress, even though the end is home: it means leaving the props and cushions that make life easy, and comfort makes cowards of us all. Yet heroic ventures, too, have their power over us; and it is a heroic thing to launch out into the infinite deep. It should hearten us to reflect on the witness of those who have set out before us and have reached the goal: that at the end there are a peace and a joy that surpass understanding as they defy expression, and that even in the early stages, if we embark on them with complete readiness of will, there is to be found, despite all the difficulties, the joy of liberation and of the discovery of life's real meaning, the joy that comes from the entry into infinite life.

But we must look more closely at this voyage of discovery: in what exactly does it consist? Some people think that if they can swoon with delight at the sight of a buttercup they are somehow in tune with the Infinite; they may be, but they are not thereby men of prayer. Some think that if the singing of a hymn fills them with warmth they are men of prayer; but they may well be mistaken. Some think that prayer, at least as we find it in the saints, is something odd and rather unhealthy; a question of morbid psychic experiences: it is not. Some again think that being a man of prayer means being a dreamer, absent-minded and unpractical; and they too are mistaken. Men of prayer are hard-bitten realists: they say in effect, God is what is most real and true and good and beautiful, so much so that everything else if viewed apart from him is unimportant and shallow; and we know what we have to do that he may show himself to us, and we are going to do it, and nothing under the sun will stop us.

I am sure, said St. Paul, that neither death nor life, nor angels nor principalities nor powers, neither things present nor things to come, neither height nor depth nor any other creature, shall be able to separate us from the charity of God. The artist and the lover—and we are all meant to be artists and lovers in one way or another—see beauty and love it and feel compelled to serve it. The man of prayer sees perfect beauty, and nothing will prevent him from serving that, to the end of his days and the last drop of his blood.

The voyage of discovery is a voyage to discover love; and the end therefore is union. But the union of lovers, as we have seen, is a thing that takes a lifetime to achieve. And this voyage of discovery which is prayer, this above all takes a lifetime to achieve. It need not involve anything extraordinary or dramatic; it need not involve strange psychic powers or psychic experiences; but it must certainly involve hard work and patience and perseverance. How are we to set about the task?

To fit ourselves for any strenuous way of life there are two things that we must do. First we must concentrate upon it, schooling ourselves to sacrifice interests or pursuits which would clash with it; forming our characters so as to be able to meet the demands it will put upon us. Secondly we must form our minds: we shall need to be humble enough to learn, concentrated enough to be able to practise what we have learnt, single-minded enough not to be always distracted. The more strenuous the life, the more intensive our efforts need to be. The life of prayer is not a pleasant hobby or a childish pastime: all the masters assure us of that; it is something we all ought to do, all can do, all must do if we want to be fully alive; but where the fullness of this life is concerned, while all are called, few are chosen; and few are chosen because few of us want to be chosen. Comfort makes cowards of us all.

The voyage is arduous and exacting; but the christian should feel strong, not in his own power and resources, but in the strength of Christ the Way. The aim of the christian men of prayer is not to substitute the humanity of Christ for the Godhead as the object of worship; the Church in its liturgy prays through Christ to God; the christian journey is summed up in the old phrase, *per humanitatem ad divinitatem,* through the humanity to the divinity. We are bidden to put on Christ; and then, living in his life and his power, we shall find the way to union with the Godhead, living *with* Christ *in* God. That is the path the christian saints have followed; and it is that that has given them their simple humility, their homeliness, their love and care for the small things of the world, their practical good sense, their immense energy in serving humanity. It is that too that gives them their courage; for they say, as St. Paul said, I can do all things in him who strengtheneth me.

Let us look then at the first of the two things we have to do, the forming of our characters. A man who devotes his whole life to curing disease cannot also devote his whole life to music. There is no reason why he should not love music; there is every reason why he should; but he must be prepared to give up a great deal of enjoyment of music for the sake of his calling. Where the man of prayer is concerned—and therefore where the duty of every christian is concerned—all the good things of life are like music to the doctor: he must be prepared to give up his enjoyment of them if need be for the better service of God.

Some men of prayer have indeed rejected the world altogether as evil; but that is not the way of those who follow Christ, who came to save and serve the world. On the contrary, the more they love God the more they love the world he made and redeemed. But their love is not the selfish grasping thing it is for most of us; it is not possessive. They have learnt to love things in themselves, not for what they can get out of them. They have learnt to love things in God, as part of their love of God, instead of trying to treat them as creatures of their own.

Living as they do as though in eternity, to which all things are equally present, they are not dismayed by the passing of earthly things, the restless waves of time. Living as they do in God in whom are all things, they are not dismayed by temporal loss or separation. Sorrow, yes, in full measure; but not despair. Love, but not greed. We whose motive is so often selfishness tire ourselves out with agitation and anxiety: we find ourselves in a fever of fear lest what we want should be denied us or taken from us; and our wants increase with the years and hang about our necks and make life ever less of a delight and more of a burden. Too often we love things only for the pleasure or profit or power they can give us, treating them as means, so that our vision fades; and so we are like misers, never at peace. These others love better than we: they do not grasp and clutch and cling. So there is always in them a deep undercurrent of joy. In them is fulfilled that poverty of spirit to which all the riches of the kingdom are promised; and to acquire that poverty of spirit, the ability to care and not to care—the exact opposite of what worldliness teaches us—is the first of the things we have to do.

Then there is the adventure of the mind itself. Here too we have to learn the exact opposite of what the world teaches us; for the world thinks of truth as something to be grasped and possessed and wrenched to our uses; but the wise men tell us that it is something to be wooed in silence and humility, something to be possessed by, if we are worthy, and something which, if we are worthy, may make use of us. The depths of reality are revealed to us, the abyss

of the human heart is filled, only by waiting in stillness on
the voice and presence of God; learning indeed to see him
and reverence him in all things, but also withdrawing ourselves at times from every activity and interest and laying
bare our minds and hearts to his touch. That quiet seeking for the Infinite for a short time every day: that is the
essential. Prayer is asking, yes; it is living our cares and
loves in God's sight and offering them to him, yes; but it
is more than that. It is the relentless effort, in spite of
difficulty and fatigue and failure, to come closer to him,
to fill ourselves with his presence, and so gradually to come
to know him and be with him in a silence like the silent
communion of lovers. Then he in his turn can speak and
enlighten our darkness; can come, and tarry with us; until
at the end we are one with him, we are in eternity though
we walk the roads of England, we live in his life and act
in his power, we are fully, completely, because divinely,
alive, because we can say as St. Paul said, I live, now not I,
but Christ liveth in me.

Chapter 13: PRAYER AND POLITICS (II)

We have seen something of the nature and necessity of
prayer; and now it remains to ask the final question: what
exactly has it to do with politics?

For some people the two worlds of prayer and politics
stand in direct opposition; there can be no question of
passing from the one world to the other; prayer means for
them a flight from activity, and if it attempts to pass over
into the world of activity it destroys itself. This is an
eastern view of prayer; it is not the christian view. Indeed
in christian eyes it is the great mistake of the East, as
activism is the great mistake of the West. The christian
ideal is neither action without prayer nor prayer without

action, but prayer overflowing into action. And the reason why is not difficult to see. Let us put it in three points.

First, the christian holds that the world about him is a real world of real things and real persons, made by God and loved by God but fallen on evil days. Then, secondly, he believes that God so loved the world that he took upon himself our humanity to heal it, so that all men should be won back in him and through him to life and sanity and peace. And, thirdly, the prayerful christian not only knows about God, he knows God: he has the knowledge that begets love and is begotten of love; and because love means union of wills—we *want* to do the will of those we love—he is driven to work for the fulfilment of God's desire, he cannot but try to help and serve the world; and the more he is filled with the life of God, the more he will love the world and dedicate himself to serving it.

We may well be tempted to run away from a world that is blind and insane; but if we do we may be running away from our duty and our destiny. The zest for social action which characterizes the West is diseased because it is not founded on vision; yet something of greatness clings to it, for there still clings to it something of love. But if you separate one law from another on which it depends, the first will go awry. We have tried to separate the love of man from the love of God; and so the love of man becomes weak or sour in us; it turns into the ineffectiveness of un-directed energy, or of sentiment, or even finally into a form of the love of self.

The christian men of prayer tell us that the first thing is to find God and cleave to him; but they tell us too that when we find him we shall find a boundless power and energy, the power and energy of God himself. That is why these men of prayer are usually something more than hard-headed realists: they are severely practical people.

They found hospitals and schools, and run them with homely efficiency; they sweep away social abuses; they carry out schemes of social reform. And there is one thing in particular in which they differ from those uncomfortable people who are reformers without being men of prayer: not only is there nothing about them of the coldness and condescension which make social service an insult, but much more than that, they change not merely the outward shape of things but the inward lives and hearts of men and women as well. Elizabeth Fry did not only reform the prison system; she restored hope and joy and love to the brutalized people in the prisons.

That is why we need the men of prayer. We need them because they can show us what is true; but we need them too because they can win us over to what is good. (It is worth noting that a taste for discussing life-and-death problems as though they had no bearing on our own lives is one of the signs that a society is dying; the pursuit of action without vision is another; and both these things are characteristic of the contemporary world: we have no time to lose if we work for the recovery of the West.) Too often what might have been a united and therefore successful effort to build a better world is broken up by envy and jealousy and vanity and suspicion, individual or national: the men of prayer shed these ugly things, their whole desire is to be instruments not for their own purposes but for God's, and so they go gently and firmly on, unworried about what the result may be, leaving that to God—and the work gets done. Or it may be that we give up and abandon the struggle, in cynical despair of ever storming the citadels of entrenched privilege: but the men of prayer have a faith and a perseverance sufficient to move even these human mountains. Again it may be simply that sloth and self-interest make us deaf to the cry of the world;

A.H.

so it was that when Leo XIII drew up what is called in English the *Workers' Charter,* denouncing the social evils of the times and sketching the outlines of a just social order, his call for action produced little effect even among those who acknowledged his authority. In a prayerful society, the toleration of such evils would be unthinkable.

The truth is that we always tend to take on the temper of mind of the world we live in. Sloth and selfishness are part of our human nature as we know it; but since the days when Europe began to reject the christian faith people have tended more and more to assume that selfishness—enlightened self-interest—is the right and proper thing for the individual. We have forgotten more and more that we are a family. A man-centred world very quickly becomes a self-centred world, and a self-centred world is a world in danger; but a world which has persuaded itself that it is right to be self-centred is doomed indeed. And it is all too possible for christians themselves to absorb this temper of mind; and to enact a sort of spiritual version of it, seeking to obey God outwardly indeed, but in a self-centred and self-interested way, embarking on a career of spiritual money-making and closing the bowels of their compassion, as St. John says, to their brethren. If we do that we deny our faith in the very act of righteously affirming it; for God is love, and only he who abides in love abides in God. To pretend to love God while having no concern for our brother-men, no concern for anyone but ourselves, is to make a mockery of love. It is a terrible thing to betray Christ; but the most terrible thing in the world is to betray Christ with a kiss.

Now if it is true that prayer, so far from being a denial of action, urges us to action, are we right in saying that it is true in particular of political action? Was the Grey Eminence attempting the impossible, the contradictory,

when he tried to live in both worlds and to serve God in
both worlds? [1] The question is only one of many similiar
questions which face the man seeking to serve God in a sin-
laden world. There are those, for instance, who have set
themselves, not to combat the evils of industrialism from
without, but to redeem industrialism from within; and
they are surely right, they are following in the footsteps of
him who became man that he might redeem humanity as
a whole from within. You cannot do that which is in
itself evil; you cannot engage in a sinful form of commerce,
in financial trickery, in warfare which is unjustifiable, and
then quieten your conscience by claiming that you are
attempting to redeem the sin from within. But the world
of politics is not necessarily evil in itself. It can indeed be
sordid and inhuman; it can be a world of trickery and greed;
it can be based on the principle that might is right; but it
need not be any of those things. The alternative was
described for us many centruies ago by one of the greatest
of the Greeks, the idea of a political system built on the
ideas of right and wrong, the ideal of the king who should
have both wisdom and power, and being wise should
know the true and the good, and being king should be
able to shape the life of society accordingly, and it has not
always been allowed to remain a wholly unrealized dream.
Where there is no vision the people perish: that the man of
vision, the man of prayer, should feel urged to do what he
can to help in the realization of this ideal, either by com-
bating the world of politics from without if it is wholly
evil, or redeeming it from within if it is not wholly evil but
labouring, like other human enterprises, under the weight
of human stupidity and blindness: that is only what we
should expect from the definition of the christian life of
prayer.

[1] Cf. Appendix A, below.

But the fact remains that there is a special danger, and the life of the Grey Eminence makes it plain. The christian man of prayer does not leave the world of politics to its fate lest he be contaminated, for he relies on God's power, not on his own: love is the motive and love drives out fear: he is in the world to serve the world, and you do not serve the world by running away from it. But on the other hand there is the danger: you do not serve God but rather betray him if you attempt to achieve his purposes by the use of evil means; and there is no lack of examples in christian history of men who have sought to serve God and have acted in good faith and with good will, but have in fact done evil where they sought to do good, have denied Christ when they thought to follow him. We cannot fight for truth with the weapons of falsehood, we cannot serve love with the weapons of hatred and evil.

Democracy lays a heavy burden on the shoulders of the individual. For if we translate the Greek ideal of the king who is both seer and ruler into democratic terms it means that all must be wise since all have power. That is why political changes will be of little avail unless many people set out to change themselves by the method of the men of prayer. The men of prayer are the ones who help to save; if we fail to be like them, or at least to be taught and energized by them, it looks very much as though we must count ourselves among the destroyers.

What then are the main lines of reconstruction as they must appear to christian men of prayer, and what do they mean to us as individuals? We could say that there are two principles on which the whole social structure must be based: first, it is the human person that is of supreme importance on earth since the human person alone has a divine destiny; and every man and woman has this destiny, so that in this respect all are equally important, there are no class distinctions in the kingdom of God. Secondly, the human being is made perfect through the love of God and therefore through serving the human family which is God's family; so that, as one great man of prayer expressed it, all our life should be work, and all our work should be work for others.

Now at first sight these two things might seem contradictory. According to the first, society is for the individual; according to the second, the individual is for society. And if you think of the two as separate, they are indeed contradictory. We have seen a social order based on the principle that society is for man: and it is simply ordered selfishness. We have seen a social order based on the principle that man is for society, the State: and it is simply ordered tyranny. But if you put the two things together you have neither selfishness nor tyranny: you have a family.

The happy family is one in which things are so arranged that the children may become good, wise, mature men and women. But they will only become such if, all the time, they work for each other, help one another, love and reverence one another—in a word, serve the family. Let charity make thee a slave, said Augustine, since truth has made thee free. We become fully men through loving service. It is the same when we think of men and women in the national family; or of nations in the human family. If we think only of the rights of men or nations we get selfishness, and therefore chaos; if we think only of duties, we get tyranny. If we put them together we get fullness of life in the unity and peace of the family.

Let us look first of all at the rights. There are some things which belong to man by the very fact that he is a human being. Every man has a right to live; and a social order which reduces some of its members to starvation is an unjust social order. He has a right to think his own thoughts, to obey his conscience, to worship God; otherwise he would be living not a human but a sub-human life. He has a right to marry and found a family, because this again is part of human life as such; and a social order in which people find that through no fault of theirs they just have not enough money to marry or have children is an unjust social order. He has a right to provide for his future and his family's future; for he cannot live a dignified human life, free, stable, assured, if he lives in constant insecurity. He has a right, too, to the dignity and happiness of creative and responsible work; if we are prevented from devoting our lives to some form of making we are not living a full human life, and a social order which so prevents us is an unjust social order. Now we could sum up all these rights by saying that every man has a right to make his own life; to be a complete human being, and the reason is that he is destined to love God, and only a complete human being, free and responsible, can love God without hindrance. The whole purpose of a social order, then, is to preserve and foster a man's enjoyment of these rights, to help him to make his own life for God.

But every right implies a corresponding duty. The rights we claim from others we must acknowledge in others: the help we claim from others we must give to others. We must serve the common good; and be ready if need be to sacrifice our own interests for it. And as the needs of society may grow greater, even perhaps to the point of having to meet a threat to its very existence, so its claims upon us will be the greater, even perhaps to the point of asking us to sacrifice our very lives. Yet even then, when the principle of man-for-society is at fullest stretch, the principle of society-for-man is at fullest stretch too; we become fully men through loving service; and to lay down one's life for one's friends is a perfect work.

We cannot examine here the sort of detailed programme which, in our circumstances, might best fulfil the christian ideal. But there is one immediate application of the idea of community which it may be well to note. A great deal of harm can be done by talking loosely of the Church condemning communism and upholding private property, without explaining exactly what is meant. In the first place the Church does not condemn communism: on the contrary, it regards one type of communism—the voluntary communism of monks and nuns—as a counsel of perfection. Secondly, the Church does condemn the evils of marxist communism, as it condemned those of nazism; but it does not thereby ally itself with the evils of capitalism. On the contrary, those evils have stood condemned by the Church for a very long time. And one of those evils is a quite un-christian idea of private property.

The Church upholds the right to ownership, yes; but not as the term is nowadays understood. No one is absolute owner of anything, except God. We are only stewards. Legally a man may do what he chooses with his own; but not morally. He may not use his property against the common good; he may not waste it; he may not use it to injure his neighbour; he must use it to help his neighbour when his neighbour is in need. The miserly and irresponsible ideas we tend to fall into about property: *these* are the direct opposite of the teaching of the Church. We have been thinking of the christian attitude towards material things; and we find that christian spirit applied to property, not in those who stand by their rights and hold to what is theirs while the rest of the world may starve, but most perfectly in those early christians who held all things in common, in St. Paul who speaks of having nothing and possessing all things, in St. Francis who took the lady Poverty for his bride, and in his friend St. Dominic, who on his deathbed bade his followers, Possess poverty.

The Church upholds the right to private property; but again, not as the term is nowadays understood. It affirms that every man has a right to security from penury or want; a right to possess enough to enable him to live a dignified human life. But nowadays—and it is a striking criticism of our society—nowadays the term man of property means, not what all men are by their common right as men, but what a few men are by particular privilege. Nowadays the word property suggests to us not the poor man's cottage or plot of land so much as the rich man's rents and dividends. And here the Church speaks very differently. It speaks not of rights so much as of duties; its purpose is not to defend so much as to warn. If we take the christian assertion of the rights of the poor and turn it into a defence of riches without responsibility, or of wealth battening upon poverty and powerlessness; or if we try to make it an argument for leaving undisturbed a grossly unequal distribution of wealth; then we are just playing on words; and what we are really upholding is not the Church's teaching at all but a travesty of it. Indeed, we are turning it completely inside out: we are using it to destroy the very thing the Church sets out to defend: justice, and to defend the very injustices it sets out to destroy.

So too with a system founded purely on the profit-motive and on cut-throat competition. There is nothing wrong necessarily with the profit-motive; there is everything wrong with a system whose one guiding principle is the profit-motive. It is more than fifty years since Leo XIII spoke in words of fire of the greed of unchecked competition, of rapacious usury, and of how a very few rich men had been able to lay upon the labouring masses a yoke little better than slavery; yet still the profit system is often regarded as sacred. The alternative, production for use, production for the common good—and this need not exclude a just profit—is simple commonsense; and would spare us the tragic insanity of want and unemployment in a world of plenty. It is simple commonsense; it is also simple christianity. It was Christ who taught us that if we want to be happy we must serve our fellow men; and it was not the authors of the Communist Manifesto who first said, If a man will not work, neither let him eat; it was St. Paul.

We have been thinking so far of our national life; but all this applies equally to the life of the world. Nations, like individuals, have rights to be respected; and each has its different contribution to make to the common good. They too have to avoid the twin dangers of tyranny over weaker nations and of the selfishness which leads to cut-throat competition, to living solely by the profit-motive, instead of serving the world. If all this is true, then there is one very practical moral we might draw and think about. Love unites; hatred divides. The one sure way of keeping the world in chaos is to draw up plans for it with hatred in our hearts. These are days when many find it hard not to hate. But there has been only one man who could say with truth, I have conquered the world; he is the God of love; and he said it on the way to the Cross.

Let us return once again to the root of the matter. Where there is no vision the people perish. At the beginning of the greatest series of events in the whole of history you find the words of a woman, Behold the handmaid of the Lord: be it done to me according to thy word. There you have indeed the picture of a contemplative, of one who has vision. Would you have expected that the announcement of the spirit messenger would be followed immediately by an immense activity, an immense bustle of planning and preparation? No, her Son was to spend thirty years in hidden silence before his active life; and all the saints who followed him were to do something of the same. Before the action the contemplation, the long quiet period of prayer and the inner preparation of the will. Her will indeed is made perfect already; she is without sin; she can even now make her acceptance absolute because she is even now living wholly in love—that perfect love that turns all the desires of the will into one single desire, and transmutes that single unified will into the Will of him who is loved: *fiat mihi*, be it done according to thy word. Yet for her too there is first the stillness:

> He came al so stil
>> Where his mother lay;
> Like dew in April
>> That falleth on the spray;

she kept all these words in her heart, we are told a little later on: kept them in her heart to ponder them, assimilate them, understand more and more of what they meant for mankind. Her will perfect in love; but still there is the need of a deeper and deeper assimilation of this new thing, a deeper and deeper dedication to its demands. Then she will be ready; then the time for action will have come.

If we could say fully and absolutely, Thy will be done, we should be saints: it is the stuff of holiness. It is also the condition of perfect activity in the world. If you want to achieve anything in the world you must have power; if you want to achieve anything real and deep and lasting you must have inner power, the power that is synonymous not with having or doing but with being. If you want to teach you must have the truth: that is the first essential; and if you can expound the truth you can do good even though you yourself are not good, for God writes straight with crooked lines; but it is all too easy for a listener to hear and perhaps be convinced, perhaps be moved, and then go away and forget. Of our Lord we are told on the other hand that he spoke with power, power went forth from him; and the same is true in degree of the saints. You do not forget so readily what they have said—perhaps indeed you are a completely different being after they have spoken to you—because the truth is not merely something that they have but something that they are: they have become it and are made one with it by the power of love; and because the truth is God it is God who fills them and whose power is in them, and you feel it radiating from them and shining from their eyes. It is because the saint can say, I live, now not I but Christ, that he can add with the proud humility of selfless love, I can do all things. . . .

Action is thus conditioned by contemplation. First you must be whole; then you can make whole in the power of that divine wisdom of which we are told that it is more active than all active things. To state it thus is of course to state the ideal; for most of us a distant approximation, a feeble attempt to illumine activity by some measure of vision, an attempt to match our fumbling efforts to do good by equally fumbling efforts to gain a little more insight, is all that can be looked for. Yet the fact is clear: one of the main causes of scandal and tragedy in the Church's life has always been the attempt on the part of some of its members to achieve good ends by means which at worst were downright evil, at best material and worldly, the way of men without vision. We are to rely, in the words of the psalmist, not on chariots and horses but on the name of the Lord. It does not mean that we are to make no provision, no use of material things; far from it. But what is so noticeable about the men of prayer is their quiet refusal to be perturbed or cast down when resources fail them, and on the other hand their rejection of any plan or endeavour that does not spring from a complete subjection to the will of God, that will which their vision reveals to them. Use your chariots and horses, their lives tell us, if God sends you chariots and horses; but if he withholds them, never mind, he will see that you reach your goal. And if you are to have them, then never forget that it is God who holds the reins: you will end in disaster if you once decide that it is you who are to drive.

Contemplation is the condition of action because it is only by learning to live with God that we can hope to achieve the complete union of the will with God; and it is only by achieving that complete union with God that we can be filled with his power and share fully in the redemptive activity of Christ in the world.

Perhaps we tend to foreshorten unjustifiably the horizon of that redemptive activity in the world: to think of the apostolic life and its attempt to pass on the vision of truth in terms simply of an appeal to the *minds* of men—and to minds capable of seeing clearly, judging objectively, and acting upon what they have seen and judged. In fact, the Church is faced with something much mightier, the mystery of iniquity which operates within the world of man; and with something much more complex and unpredictable than pure reason, that human mind which is swayed by emotion and prejudice and is itself the battleground of the cosmic forces of good and evil. This perhaps we tend to forget; and so we forget too that only those who speak and work in the power of Christ can do fully in the world the will of Christ.

Blessed are the poor in spirit, the beatitudes tell us; blessed are the clean of heart; blessed are the meek. The substance of the three counsels of perfection is not something confined to the cloister but something which is meant to live in every christian. For it is the same essential lesson which they express.

You must be poor in spirit whatever your status and fortune in the world: it means that you must learn not to clutch and grasp at things and regard them as your creatures to be used simply for your profit and pleasure; you must reverence things because they are God's handiwork and his omnipresence makes them holy; then you may use them, but not as their master, not as if they were yours. You must, in other words, have vision.

You must be clean of heart: it means not only that you must be temperate, trying to restore the will of the flesh to its proper creative function in the whole personality, trying to make passion the expression and not the destruction of love and unity; but also that you must learn through obedience to the Spirit to see and judge *quasi oculo Dei,* as though with the eyes of God, with the wisdom which is clearer and purer than even the deepest and most unbiassed human wisdom can be because, as the *Book of Wisdom* tells us, it is a certain pure emanation of the glory of the almighty God. So again you must have vision.

You must be meek; and here you have the summary of the way of holiness, the summary of the way of the men of prayer. You must be humble; which means that you must reverence and accept the truth, neither belittling your gifts nor regarding them as your handiwork or your own property; having the carefree courage and strength of the saints in defending the truth, sharing the carefree peace and strength of the saints in their indifference to attacks upon themselves. It means therefore that you must worship and serve the truth with the stillness of soul that is in Mary's *fiat*: you must be a contemplative, you must have vision.

Whenever there is question of doing great work for God there is always the danger of becoming so absorbed in the work itself, in choice of ways and means, in calculation of success and failure, that you tend to forget the end in view and consequently to spoil the work by robbing it of its poverty and chastity and obedience. Whatever the enterprise may be there is only one true and final end, his will. Of course we think in terms of immediate success and failure; of course we are sad if we fail; but if we have begun in the spirit of Mary's *fiat* we shall not be discouraged because we shall know that the failure is not final—there is never failure where there is fulfilment of God's will. The model for us is not the glittering immediate success which Satan proposed to Christ in the desert, but the folly and seeming failure of the Cross. The work of God is done in deeper ways than we know—unless we are men of vision indeed; and success is often failure and failure often success, for the life of the Church is like the seed growing secretly. Poverty, chastity, obedience, are all forms of detachment; and detachment is the fruit of vision; for it means the ability to love with all the strength of one's soul and at the same time be ready to surrender all the things that one loves into the hands of God, who loves them better still. That is why if we want to work for the world we must try to be contemplatives; that is why it is true that where there is no vision the people perish; that is why political changes of themselves can be of little avail; for it is only by being men of prayer that we can hope to share in that *fiat* which is the condition of redemptive activity as it is the condition of poverty and joy and peace of soul: only so can we hope to have something of that inner power which is the fruit of love and wisdom, the power that is born in stillness and that works in stillness, and that like the dew in April that falleth on the spray cannot fail to bring solace and refreshment and renewal to the parched soil of the world.

Appendix A

THE RECENT WORK OF MR. ALDOUS HUXLEY

Where there is no vision the people perish ... The mystics are channels through which a little knowledge of reality filters down into our human universe of ignorance and illusion. A totally unmystical world would be a world totally blind and insane. From the beginnings of the eighteenth century onwards, the sources of all mystical knowledge have been steadily diminishing in number, all over the planet. We are dangerously far advanced into the darkness.[1]

For several centuries now Europe has been the battle-ground for an attack upon the very existence of the spirit of man, though it was during and after the eighteenth century that the attack reached its height; and it is man who has been more or less consistently the loser until almost the whole of his heritage has been taken from him. The stature of christian man was infinite—we speak of christian doctrine and belief not practice, *quia omnes nos peccavimus*: we betray what we believe but that does not invalidate the beliefs—because seeking first the kingdom of heaven he could find oneness with God and be fillled, and all the other things, the knowledge and love of created things and joy in them, and the whole of a happy human life, were added to him. He was a thing of majesty because he was God's child. But the New Order of the Renaissance did away with the grandeur and humility of christian man; and substituted for them the abasement and pride of finite man, of man the measure of all things, of man in the loneliness and isolation of his own self hood remote from God. That isolation is the stuff of hell; for

[1] Aldous Huxley: *Grey Eminence*, p. 82.

hell is not in its essence a punishment wrought upon man, but the state of being without Being which man inflicts upon himself; and all the ugliness and shame and squalor which are in the world are only the manifestation of that isolation and rootlessness which creation inflicted upon itself and which in the ultimate doom is made permanent. But for a time man remained unaware that he was in hell: there was so much beauty on the surface of life and within the confines of the natural man-measured world. The dream was not allowed to last, however, for the eighteenth century stripped man of all the beauty and awareness that were incompatible with rationalism: as far as philosophy is concerned, the Age of Enlightenment was a dark alley peopled with thinking machines. The nineteenth century denied even the higher ambitions of reason: it denied man's power to know reality and at the same time taught him that he was the puppet of a mechanist universe and that the miseries which industrialism had brought upon him were therefore without redress. And in these latter days we have seen the squalid end of the process of impoverishment, wherein reason is denied altogether and man is totally deprived of his personality and reduced to a capacity only for blind instinctive responses to the demands of a pseudo-absolute. Those political leaders in the contemporary world who still hold to something better than this or have been aroused by its horror to a remembrance of something better than this have more to do than win a military victory over it; for if they beckon us back to the world of economic man as the fruits of victory, or, what is more likely and more disastrous, plunge us in our turn into the abyss of totalitarian subhumanity, they may well find that human endurance has no further limits; and then the battle for the soul of man will be over and will have ended in total defeat.

The question we have to ask with heavy misgiving is whether they can reasonably be expected to do otherwise or at least to do much better. The worlds of politics and religion are by now so completely sundered that it may well be thought wildly improbable that the one should heed the other. Yet, asks Mr. Huxley, what can the politicians 'do for their fellows by actions within the political field, and without the assistance of the contemplatives'? 'The answer would seem to be: not very much.' The modern West is the one historical civilisation which has been stupid enough to suppose that action without contemplation can be productive of good; and even in face of the shambles to which its belief has led it there is little enough reason to expect a radical change: it is always easy to find a scapegoat for misfortune and to ignore the conditions which produced the scapegoat. So we may expect more political action obedient to the formulas of enlightened self-interest and therefore productive of not very much. 'Political reforms cannot be expected to produce much general betterment unless large numbers of individuals undertake the transformation of their personality by the only known method which really works—that of the contemplatives.' In Mr. Huxley's view it is idle to expect any such transformation in the world of to-morrow; for 'technological progress, nationalism and war seem to guarantee that the immediate future of the world shall belong to various forms of totalitarianism,' and totalitarianism and mysticism or theocentric religion are incompatible.

But quite apart from that, for Mr. Huxley there is an inherent incompatibility between the two worlds: the politicians are the 'brewers of poisons,' the mystics are the 'antidote-makers'; all that the former can do is to help 'to create a social environment favourable to contemplatives'

A.H.

or, at any rate, 'refrain from doing certain things and making certain arrangements which are specially unfavourable'; seer and ruler belong to different castes, and to attempt to pass from the one to the other is necessarily disastrous. Contemplation is what matters; and contemplation—the point was made very clearly by Mr. Propter in *After Many a Summer*—is the negation of social action, the unmasking of its futility.

Fr. Joseph, the *Eminence Grise,* is a tragically fascinating example of a man who tried to achieve the ideal of the philosopher-king, a contemplative who became a politician. He failed; and ended only by degrading his contemplation and doing evil in the political world. His history raises absorbing and tantalising questions: how did he come to enter the political world at all; how could he accept the power politics of his time apparently without scruple; how could he imagine his two particular worlds to be compatible? These questions are dealt with in Mr. Huxley's brilliant study of the man; but it is the general questions which lie behind these, and with which Mr. Huxley is really concerned, that are of greater moment. Is the ideal of the philosopher-king a chimera? Is the nature of contemplation such that it cannot issue in action without destroying itself, cannot even be reconciled with the world of action? Does religion betray itself if it intrudes into the world of affairs?

The answers we give to these questions must depend upon what we mean by contemplation and by politics; and it is here that Mr. Huxley's argument demands most careful scrutiny. For him, the Church is faithful to the 'Dionysian tradition' of mysticism until the eighteenth century; then, with Bérulle and his associates, there comes a revolution in the theology and practice of mysticism, a revolution which in fact hastens the destruction of contemplation itself; and the attack upon the quietists, once one has got beneath its surface justifications, is revealed as part of the conscious or unconscious assault by ecclesiastics upon mysticism itself. The 'Bérullian revolution' takes an important place among the causes which produced the practical disappearance of mysticism from the Church from the end of the seventeenth to the end of the nineteenth centuries because it changed the object of contemplation, substituting for the Unknowable the Humanity of Christ and the Passion, and so precluding the real aim of contemplation which is union with ultimate Reality.

Now there is a considerable confusion here which calls for comment, for it goes to the root of the matter. It may be noted in passing, in the first place, that Benet Fitch's book was frowned upon for its quietist simplifications, so that he can hardly be bracketed with the 'over-orthodox' Bérulle. Secondly, and more important, it is a strange distortion to present the relatively unimportant Bérulle as the initiator of a revolution in mystical teaching. There have been throughout the history of the Church in the West two streams of mystical theory and practice: the one (the 'Dionysian') in which the accent is on the *via negativa*, the mysticism of the 'cloud of unknowing'; the other (the 'Gregorian'), which is more active, practical and personal, and which in later days, under the influence especially of the Ignatian school, evolved a technique of meditation or pre-mystical prayer which assumed great importance in the times with which Mr. Huxley is here concerned. Now it may well be that over-emphasis on this technique, with its dangers of self-consciousness and activism, did in fact lead to a decline in mysticism—in view of the general temper of mind of the eighteenth century it might be expected; but it is quite unjustifiable to argue from this that the aim of the two ways of contemplation differed and that the Bérullian school substituted the incarnate Christ for the Godhead. On the contrary, in this respect there has been but one way of prayer throughout the Church's history: the way which is summed up in the words of the *De Adhaerendo Deo, per humanitatem ad divinitatem,* through the Humanity to the Godhead, and in the words of the Church's liturgy which prays not *ad Christum* but *per Christum.* This is the process which all christian mystics of whatever age or school have followed; which is why, for example, an exponent of the method of the Bérullian St. John Eudes speaks of his view of prayer as 'profoundly theocentric,' and why Evelyn Underhill quotes from Bérulle himself when showing that Christocentric worship 'when rightly understood [is] not an alternative to pure theistic devotion but a special form of it.'[1] When therefore Mr. Huxley tells us that the 'contemplatives of the Dionysian tradition . . . had adapted dogma to their own experience, with the result that, in so far as they were advanced mystics, they had ceased to be specifically christian,' one can only say that it would be very

---

[1] *Cf.* C. Lebrun: *The Mystical Teaching of St. John Eudes,* p. 133; E. Underhill: *Worship,* p. 69. The mystics with whom Mr. Huxley deals are mainly concerned with the lower (introductory) stages of the mystical life; Fr. Joseph himself for example was concerned in his teaching with the prayer of quiet; there was no departure from tradition in associating these forms of prayer with the Passion—has not the very 'Dionysian' Tauler left us Meditations on the Passion?—and equally certainly there was no intention of substituting these introductory stages for mystical prayer itself. The ascent of Mount Carmel demands a technique, intellectual as well as moral; it may be held that this particular sort of technique is too cerebral or too 'busy' to achieve its object perfectly, or that those who taught it in the days of Fr. Joseph put so much emphasis upon it as to obscure its object; but the main point here is that neither they nor their technique set out to obscure that object, and that the possession of the objective by the highest mystics in its turn does not exclude, but on the contrary implies, active concern for the redeemed world and its Redeemer.

hard to prove his contention from the life of any of the great christian mystics. The christian is concerned first to put on Christ and then, living in him, to find the fulfilment of the Christ-life in union with the Godhead—hidden *with* Christ *in* God. The Incarnation, with all that it implies of charity, of action in and for the world, is not something that the mystic outgrows, but something that he responds to, assimilates, fulfils in himself, by union with the Godhead. And because the heights of mysticism are thus the realisation of the Incarnation they are precisely what Mr. Huxley would have them not to be: they are not the denial and rejection of the world, of action, of fellowship and service, but the implicit affirmation of them, an affirmation which of its own energy will overflow into action of the most practical sort.

It has indeed been remarked that what differentiates the great mystics from the psychopaths is precisely their zest and ability for doing good: St. Teresa, with her numerous religious foundations and her general air of motherly good sense, is an obvious example. We may recall the wise words of M. Maritain: 'This activism and pragmatism [of the West] are, so to say, the catastrophe of something which is very great indeed, but which the spirit of separation from God has jeopardised: the catastrophe of that generosity, that propensity to give and to communicate to others, that sense of ontological superabundance, which comes from *caritas* and from holy contemplation overflowing into action. Whereas it has to be asked whether the impassable contemplation of the East . . . does not in its turn betray, in the very spiritual order itself, a pragmatism incomparably more subtle, but which none the less shirks the witness which God expects of humanity.'[1]

Christian mysticism at its highest is the fulfilment of the

[1] *Questions de Conscience*, p. 153.

Incarnation and therefore of the love of both of God and of man; and it is this fact which enables it to serve the world and may enable it even at the eleventh hour to save the world in the power and at the prompting of God. It is able to serve and to save because at the very summit of union with the Infinite and Unknowable it remains humble and homely: it is never too absorbed, too proud, to remember the little things of the world, the needs and cares and sorrows of men and women, nor to love with God the creatures he has made and redeemed and in which his glory is made manifest. It is strange that this should be obscure to Mr. Huxley with his concern for the world in which we live—so obscure apparently as to lead him into the uncharacteristic (because ill-informed and unscholarly) gibes which every now and then obtrude into his pages.[1] We are all children of a single family; and it is as a family that we are meant to return to God, the Infinite Incomprehensible who is yet the Father of us all.

Christian mysticism, then, so far from being incompatible with action, of itself impels to action. In the heart of the mystery of the mystic's union with the Unknowable he discovers the desire and energy for redemptive action which alone can win back the world to God. The salvation of the world depends upon the mystics in a way other than that which Mr. Huxley has seen. It is not enough to know the truth and tell the truth. It is indeed one of the most deeply disturbing features of our present-day world that the speculations and debates of intellectuals seem so often to be self-confined, to lack the vital energy that turns theory into reality. It is a phenomenon of a *fin-de-siècle* society.

---

[1] *E.g.* that Catholics believe in the 'magic efficacy of rites and sacraments'; that orthodox christianity has always tended to confuse 'the merely psychic with the spiritual'; that petitionary prayer is appropriate only to those whose 'religion is anthropocentric'.

But to say that christian contemplation overflows into redemptive activity is not at all the same as saying that it overflows into politics. On the other hand, unless the political world is leavened, how shall the world as a whole be healthy? We cannot ignore the political world; it will not let us. Here again Mr. Huxley seems to load the dice by speaking not of politics but of power politics. Where Fr. Joseph is concerned that is accurate enough; but not when the main issue is under discussion. There are three separate questions: (1) can a mystic enter the political arena without endangering his mysticism, even when political action is based on religious truth? (2) can he enter the arena of power-politics not in order to play his part in them, as Fr. Joseph did, but in order to combat them? (3) can he enter the arena of power-politics and play his part in them but with the idea of leavening them and, if possible, transforming them from within?

To the first question the answer is surely, Yes: if St. Teresa could govern her nunneries without danger to her contemplation, another mystic of equal calibre could govern a kingdom without danger to his mysticism. To the second question, too, the answer is surely, Yes; and indeed some such activity is the logical application of Mr. Huxley's own view that the mystic is the salt without which the earth will not be salted: for the mystic will not salt the earth if he abandons all contact with the earth. It is precisely this that the papacy does in its political interventions and by its political encyclicals, setting up a vivid contrast between the world as it is, so often governed by power-politics, and the world as it might be if governed by christian principles.

And what of the third question? It is the old dilemma of mucking-in and mucking-out; it must depend for its solution not only on the special character and strength of the individual, but on the degree in which the power of Mammon is entrenched. There are times when integrity can be saved only by a flight from Egypt; but on the other hand the Incarnate Word in his mystical Body lives in and for the world, and the Church is not an ivory tower. As the christian may share in Christ's redemptive activity by taking on himself the cross of industrialism in order to redeem the world of industrialism, so too he may be called to enter the world of politics to redeem the world of politics. Dangerous, no doubt; but charity is often dangerous: was it not St. Dominic who wished to be a stone blocking the mouth of hell itself?

It remains true that political reform will be of little avail unless at the same time 'large numbers of individuals undertake the transformation of their personality' by the method of the contemplatives. To be a contemplative is thus a social as well as a personal obligation. The only practical way of government is that of the philosopher-king, though wisdom and power need not necessarily reside in a single individual provided only that power is obedient to wisdom. It is the burden which democracy places on the shoulders of the citizens that if the state is to be healthy each and all must be contemplatives, or at least aware of and obedient to the wisdom of the contemplatives in their exercise of power. The failure of Fr. Joseph was a personal failure; and does not alter the fact that the destiny of each of us is to be, in however humble a degree, philosopher-kings. The christian mystic can never outgrow the *Our Father*: the deeper his absorption in the mystery of the Godhead, the more intensely is his spirit and his whole life a prayer that the kingdom of God may *come on earth,* as it is in heaven.

It is precisely on this question of the overflow of contemplation into action that the teachings of East and West divide. Let us return from the world of politics to the more general question and the issues which underlie it—issues which Mr. Huxley's later book, *The Perennial Philosophy*, raise in an acute form. They will take us back to the nature of man; they will take us beyond that to the nature of God; and so again to the idea of union with God, and a more careful consideration of what that union is.

Mr. Huxley once wrote an essay on vulgarity in literature. But literature reflects human life; and implicitly he has written many books on vulgarity in human life, on the squalor of humanity. The figures of the fifth Earl of Gonister and his companion at the end of *After Many a Summer,* undying and unliving, intolerable in their sordid brutishness, represent something that recurs again and again in different forms in his works. 'Vivre?' he quoted in *Vulgarity in Literature,* 'nos valets le feront pour nous'. That disgust with life, and in particular with the corporeal, still seems to lie at the root of his view of reality; and to colour his approach to Reality.

Some critics of *The Perennial Philosophy* have waxed indignant at the idea of describing as philosophy a book in which Plato and Aristotle are barely mentioned; others have taken the opposite line, and vindicated the author by viewing western philosophy as pseudo-philosophy because of its exclusive reliance on discursive reasoning: if the way to knowledge of Reality is humility, poverty of spirit, purity of heart, how can we describe as philosophers, as ' lovers of wisdom', any but those who take this way? The truth surely lies midway between these two extremes. As some of the great christian mystics have shown in their own lives, there are three wisdoms: the natural investigations of reason, the study of theology, the direct mystical awareness of God; and they can each be valid and valuable in their own spheres, and each help and fortify the others. We have no right to upbraid philosophy in the western sense for not being mysticism; nor need we object if Mr. Huxley chooses to use the term in a different, but etymologically justifiable sense. What remains true is that, while western philosophy may justly be criticized for excluding the findings of mysticism from its data, this book may justly be criticized, not for failing to philosophize, but for failing to do justice to discursive reasoning in the total quest for God; and perhaps this failure links up with the author's general attitude to human life.

The Perennial Philosophy is a valuable book for many reasons. It does show the universality of the claims of mysticism; it does argue convincingly that mysticism is not a moment in the evolutionary process, a passing and primitive phase which must inevitably be superseded with the coming of greater enlightenment, but the fulfilment of something ultimate and changeless in human nature. It does, in the light of this age-old wisdom, show up the shallowness and sham of so much of our ways of thought and behaviour; it vindicates the old Greek idea of the *nemesis* which waits upon *hubris*—*hubris* in regard to nature as well as to God. It includes, in commentary as well as texts, not only the great broad lines of the Way, but a good deal of wise detail in the sphere of spiritual direction. And, in its collation of the teaching of East and West, it can do us western christians a service not least by making us more humble and less provincial, more alive to the way in which God does indeed reveal himself, in the different ages and races, to men of good will. To have brought these testimonies together, so vastly different in so many ways, so strikingly similar in the substance of their message; to have expounded and explained them so clearly; and to have revealed so clearly in the light of their wisdom the true nature of the modern world we take too much for granted and the life we too easily lead: this is no small achievement.

And yet, of its nature, this is a transitional book. It ends in an ambiguity. *Tat tvam asi*: That art thou; there is the formula, the one-ness of God and man. But what an infinity of questions it raises. What is the *That*, what is the *thou*, what is the *art*, the union between the two terms?

Mr Huxley of course has his answers; but do they take us far enough?

Let us look first of all at the human term, the *thou*. The raw material is the human personality, begotten in sin but yearning, unconsciously if not consciously, for God. What must be done in it to make it proximately *capax Dei*? The mystics reply with one voice: it must go through the process of self-naughting; and the West is as vehement as the East, and as vehement as Mr. Huxley could wish, in rejecting the 'stinking lump' of selfhood. But here already is the first major ambiguity, the first major divergence which underlies these apparently identical sayings. Mr. Huxley offers a philogical explantion of the western reverence for the idea of personality: we reject the gaunt humility of the Saxon 'selfness' and prefer the sonority of the Latin word, precisely because it bolsters up our own self- importance. Were we to speak of 'selfness' we might more readily see it to be a stinking lump. The thesis is attractively argued; but is it true? There is in fact a deep cleavage here between the teaching of christianity and that of many interpreters of the wisdom of the East. These latter command the self to die; Christ commands the self to die and be re-born. In this eastern teaching it is indeed the self that is the stinking lump and that must be totally destroyed; for the christian it is not the self but selfishness, not the true self but the false. And Mr Huxley seems to be guilty therefore of a tendencious exegesis when he changes the words of St Paul, 'I live now not I, but Christ liveth in me', to 'for it is the Logos who *lives me*—lives me as an actor lives his part'.

We are thus led to the second ambiguity. That art thou: but what is the meaning of *art*, what is the nature of the union between the two terms? And it is clear that, if we stop short at the first half of the christian formula, if what we set out to achieve is the death of the self and no more, then there cannot in fact be a union of two terms at all, since there will not in fact be two terms.

God created man to his own image and likeness. When we are trying to discover something of the love of God and man, it is wise to be humble and to examine the love of human beings for one another. That human love does in fact reveal to us the phenomenon of self-naughting: that copernican revolution which makes the centre of life—of thought and desire and effort—not the self any longer, but the other; but it also and simultaneously reveals to us that the end of that revolution is not the abolition of the self (which would mean the abolition of love with the destruction of the lover) but the discovery of the true self instead of the false.

The issue then defines itself more clearly: we are to choose between two alternatives. Either the love of wisdom is to take us to a final death of self, the result of which must not be union but absorption, the dreamless sleep, the void; or it must take us to a death which is only the gateway to rebirth, and leads therefore in the end to a real and personal union, a union of love. Which alternative corresponds to reality? We can answer only by discovering the nature of God; and so we reach the third great ambiguity.

Here we are faced at the outset with a special difficulty. The mystic is trying to express the Inexpressible; and he is therefore forced to take refuge in figurative language and paradox, and to rest content with remote approximations. It is for this reason that it is possible to interpret christian sayings in an 'absorptionist' sense ('My Me is God', said St Catherine of Genoa), and vice versa. But again the difference is as clear as it is deep. The mystics are at one in their worship of the Transcendent-Immanent, the Absolute, beyond categories, beyond understanding, the abyss of the Godhead. But what an infinity of difference, again, beneath these identities. You find intepreters of East and West alike speaking of Godhead, of God, and of Incarnation: but with what difference of implication. And it is essential that those implications should be brought out; for on them depends the whole approach, the whole attitude, of the questing soul. This Mr. Huxley recognizes: 'metaphysical thinking is unavoidable and finally necessary'; though elsewhere he asserts (very questionably: St Thomas for one did not find it so) that 'the habit of analytical thought is fatal to the intuitions of integral thinking'—and it is this latter assertion that links up with his condemnation of formulae and legalism, of christianity's 'unfortunate servitude to historical fact', its 'idolatrous preoccupation with events and things in time'. Are we back again at the vulgarity of man?

Let us be quite clear. We believe not in a creed but through a creed. We believe that doctrinal formulae can but approximate to the Fact. We believe that the world of time is immeasureably less important than the now of eternity. But we can become citizens of eternity only by using as we ought the world of time; and by using—as Mr Huxley himself admirably points out—the *minutiae*, the successive events in all their smallness, of our human lives on earth. Without dogma, worship must tend to become woolly, and the quest for God go astray into strange and sometimes sinister by-paths; there must, as Mr. Huxley admits, be a map. And how can there be a map of that which is beyond description, how can there be a formulation of that which is beyond all forms? The complete answer is that the Word was made flesh and dwelt amongst us, and in the measurable reality of human events and facts we have seen his glory, the glory of the Godhead revealed.

The *Godhead* revealed. Godhead, God, Incarnate: what is the relation between these three terms? It is not enough to say that for christianity there is but one incarnation while for buddhism there is an indefinite number: the meaning and purpose of the incarnation is different. Christ is not a man in whom God became manifest; a pattern, simply, of what man should be. The movement, so to say, is not upward, but downwards; and the purpose is not a question only of providing a pattern, but of empowering, of so changing nature as to make it capable of re-creating the pattern. Similarly, the love of the personal God is not a step on the road to the discovery of the impersonal Godhead: it is the infinite dynamic stillness of the Godhead itself that is revealed to us as comprising the mutual love of Father, Son and Holy Ghost; and that, by showing us relationship within the Absolute, shows us the possibility of a relationship *with* the Absolute, a real union, through love, of self with Self.

But again, how is the union to be achieved? If you think of incarnation as a pyschological fact but not an historical event: if you think of the love of a personal God as but a stepping-stone, as milk for babes; then perhaps inevitably you think of the mystic quest as something to be achieved by man. So indeed Mr. Huxley seems to view it: he speaks of grace, but it seems accidental rather than substantial to his thesis, and he has no use for the christian theology of the sacraments. The quest tends to become an

exclusively upward movement, and to consist in an escape
from all that is human.

But *sine me nihil potestis facere*. Without me you can do
nothing. The christian view is radically different; starts
from an entirely different angle. Christianity knows all
about the vulgarity of man, and all about the helplessness
of man; none the less it asserts roundly, 'I can do all things
. . . in him who strengthens me'. The first movement is the
downward movement of divine love and pity and healing.
The Word was made flesh; and that stooping down of
Godhead into the world of time, that historical event
which gives temporal history its eternal significance, that
is the necessary condition of man's upward movement,
and it is then indeed *man's* upward movement, not an
escape from human life, but the redeeming of human life,
even through its vulgarity, through its opacity, through
the limitations and humilations of flesh and blood; not an
escape from the self but the discovery of the self.

The Word was made flesh, and was wrapped in swaddling clothes. There is something else about the Godhead
which these historical events reveal. You think of the
vulgarity of man, the servitude to the needs and limitations and earthiness of the flesh, the squalors of egoism, the
vulnerability of existence, and it is tempting to follow the
mysticism which breaks away from it all, tempting to
think of an 'unselfing' which shall be a deliverance into
the impassibility of the One. (But God is not impassible,
because love is not impassible: he was crucified, died and
was buried.) You think of the vulgarity of ecclesiastical
man, the superstitions and sentimentalities, the degrada-
tions and the emotional wallowings into which worship
can descend; you think of the dependence on the minis-
trations of the grubby official hands in which the divine
Reality is held; and again how tempting to brush it all

aside as a man-made distraction, as a substitute and a hindrance. But no; one of the lessons that is most forcibly stated in this book is the lesson that there is no way to God except through humility of heart; and humility is the acceptance of fact, the acceptance of the facts about one-self as they are. The facts about man are that, body and soul alike, he comes from God; body and soul alike, way-ward and stupid and sinful, he is loved by God; and body and soul alike he must make his way back to God through the power that is offered him. And all that is very humilia-ting, no doubt; but it ceases at once to be humiliating if you remember the fact that 'he emptied himself, taking on himself the form of a servant,' and in that assumtion of human misery turned the misery into a glory.

He was wrapped in swaddling clothes. It changes our idea of human squalor; but it does more than that. It completes our idea of God. Let us return to the humble human example, the nature of human love. We were thinking before of that element in human love which we call tenderness, and which finds expression in the desire to protect—to protect from harm and hardship and suffering; but which in itself is an awareness which produces that desire: an awareness that you find equally in the love of man for woman and of woman for man: an awareness of dependence, of a certain helplessness, of vulnerability; an awareness that in the mature human being there still remains something of the child. Without that element of tenderness love is at best imperfect and may well be de-stroyed; and God in the infinity of his love and his pity has shown us how even here, even in our approach to the Infinite Transcendent, that tenderness is not excluded. He was wrapped in swaddling clothes. Here as elsewhere we are to go *per humanitatem ad divinitatem*: this is not essentially or even necessarily a question of devotion to the human childhood of Christ: it is a question primarily of what that childhood reveals to us of the Godhead, and of what it teaches us of the fullness of man's loving response to divine love.

If we are to worship God as our Father, how can it also be possible for us to have in our love this element of tenderness as for a child? It is possible because God has made himself vulnerable and helpless and dependent: not merely, once again, in his human childhood and its weakness, but in that divine quasi-abrogation of sovereignty whereby he leaves us to choose whether we shall love him or no. He has made himself vulnerable because he has given us free-will: he has made it possible for us to despise and reject him, as in fact we do. And to the lovers of God that aspect seems to be central: wholly different from the sentimentalities, the anthropomorphisms, the human projections, into which worship is at times degraded, you find this awareness and love in the depths of the spirit. It is for this that apostles work and suffer and die.

Metaphysical thinking is necessary. What we learn of the nature of God must determine in the last resort what we think of the nature of man. If we can think of God in this light, then we can begin to see man also in this light; we shall be concerned less with the vulgarity and more with the vulnerability of the human heart; less with the egoist squalors of the adult and more with the continuing helplessness and pathos of the child. Feed my lambs, as well as my sheep, Christ told his followers; and if we find such deep christian mysticism—as in fact we do—in so many of the simple and unlearned, it is precisely because the nature of God as self-revealed to them, and the understanding of the tragedy and pathos of man which that implies, have made it possible, have prepared and purified the heart.

A.H.

As perennial and as universal in the world's history as the mystic quest is the making of sacrifice; and here again the same lesson is clear. In sacrifice generally, and in particular in the Sacrifice which fulfils all sacrifices, there are the two movements: the offering and immolation to God, the receiving from God; and it is the self in its fullness, it is man's life together with all the things that go to make up that life, that is offered in order that, through the acceptance of the sacrifice, the self and its total setting may be restored: not an escape from squalor, but the redemption of squalor. First the death, but then the re-birth.

First the death; our Lord is quite clear: only he that hateth his life shall find it. But—hateth *his* life, not hateth life. If we want to see what his words mean we must look at the life of him who said them. He did not hate life, he did not hate the squalors of humanity, he who so loved the earth and its fullness and all the small things of the world, he who was so gentle with the weak and the timid and the sinful, while being himself so unprotected from the harshness and the crudity of human things. He did not teach us to destroy our selfhood, he who so often speaks of I and Me, for he knew that love is marriage, is a union in which not the essence but the egoism and the isolation of selfhood are transcended. Mr. Huxley resorts again to philology to point out that the idea of two-ness always involves the idea of evil; but does it? Division, yes; for division implies the privation of desired union. But two-ness need not mean the same as division: it can on the contrary mean the same as union; for without it there cannot be union, there can only be fusion and therefore destruction. Our Lord teaches us not to speak of I and Me and Mine as *we* use the words, egoistically; he teaches us to kill the false self; he teaches us to hate our own self-centred lives, because then we can learn to love and in so doing we shall discover our true lives, our true selves, the lives and selves of which the centre is the Other.

It is because of these unstated cleavages, these unresolved ambiguities, that *The Perennial Philosophy* strikes one as a transitional book. Metaphysical thinking is unavoidable; and must lead in the end to a greater definition in one direction or the other. And on that choice of direction how much depends! Christian mysticism must be defined in terms that show its care for, and redemption of, the pain and need of the world: a care that is God-like, and God-filled, because it is indeed a sharing in the very nature of Love: *In tormento e travaglia servire i fratelli.*

Appendix B

THOMIST ETHICS AND THE WORLD OF TODAY

Let us treat this title as an invitation, not to criticize the contemporary world from the point of view of thomist moral theory, but on the contrary to try to find points of contact between them, points at which perhaps thomism may supply answers to some of the questions which are vexing modern man. And let us begin therefore by enumerating some facts or tendencies which do seem to characterize the contemporary scene.

First, individualism seems to have had its day—and a long day it has been. Socialism is in the saddle; and the political landslide which put it there does seem to suggest that, underneath all the mixture and muddle of motives which determine political allegiances, there was a sense of the emptiness and evil of individualist society. On the other hand we know a good deal by now about the horrors of the collectivist, the totalitarian, alternative of whatever hue; and there is still, thank God, in the heart of the average Englishman a deep desire for the kind of political life in which he can call his soul—and his back-garden—his own. Thus modern man, consciously or unconsciously, seems to be in search of a third alternative, a synthesis to this thesis and antithesis, a kind of life which shall give him both personal fullness and freedom, and community. (A significant fact at the present time is thus, for instance, the great interest on the part of ordinary citizens in community centres.)

Secondly, in a wider political field, the doom which so obviously threatens us unless some commonly accepted way of life can be found between the nations is leading people to advert to the necessity of a natural law, to which men must subscribe *as men*, and which must form the background to, and the criterion of, political ambitions and expedients precisely because it enshrines the fundamental rights and responsibilities of human nature.

Thirdly, this last point already implies the notion of a rule of moral behaviour which is based on the idea of purpose: the idea of a natural law binding the nations means a law which describes the structure or pattern of the nations' growth in the fundamental freedoms. And when you come to personal ethics, it seems true to say that there, too, people expect a defence of moral principles to be based on some consideration of consequences. Perhaps it is arguable that an ethic which regards the rightness or wrongness of actions as something quite irrespective of their consequences could only gain acceptance in a satisfied and optimist world, where inevitable progress is taken for granted and the golden age is assumed to be round the corner. However that may be, one does find at the present time that the argument from consequences tends to take an important place in ethical discussions; one does find that the christian more and more demands (and quite rightly) a justification of this or that moral law in terms of its ability to produce happiness, or goodness, or perfection; and the same is presumably still more true of the non-christian.

Fourthly, the mention of happiness brings us to a further point. The desire for happiness is not a twentieth century phenomenon; but there is today, not unnaturally, a specially urgent though not always conscious desire to achieve the kind of happiness which attends the fulfilment of human creativity, precisely because it is so often frustrated.

But, fifthly, this sense of frustration is part of a state of soul which goes very deep. It might truly be said that restlessness is the keynote of the present age, a restlessness which is the result of tensions at various levels of the personality. (Those philosophies which abandon traditional categories of thought precisely in favour of such categories as anxiety, fear and anguish, express this characteristic of the age.) The fundamental cause of unrest in fallen man is the tension between his egocentricity and the cramping limitations and loneliness which egocentricity produces. The self can be born into fullness of life only through discovering the Other. We might distinguish four different ways in which liberation from the prison of egocentricity can be achieved and ought to be achieved by man: the way of integration through creative work, the way of integration through creative love of other individuals, the way of integration through community, and the way of integration in the life of God; and today these metaphysical needs of man are not only frustrated by the egocentricity of sin, but are blocked by particular circumstances: creative work by industrialism, creative love by the deformative influence of hollywoodism, community by the growth— open or hidden—of totalitarianism, the divine life by a surrounding atmosphere of the denial of God. It should be added that the metaphysical unrest which is the natural desire for God is intensified by the ethical unrest which is

the sense of sin; and when this too is robbed of its proper
catharsis, by humanism and optimism, or existentialism,
or any of the theories which reject theology, it is not surprising that there should follow the psychological unrest
which is expressed in terms of neurosis.

Sixthly, then, and lastly: the creative needs of man demand a creative ethic; there will be something hopelessly
unreal and unconvincing about a moral theory which
speaks only in terms of static rightness or wrongness.
For an ethic to carry conviction it must surely speak
in dynamic terms, in terms of movement and growth,
in terms of life. But at the same time it certainly cannot
be just a bland eudaemonism: a theory which paints
the moral life in terms of a smooth and effortless fulfilment of the powers and capabilities of human nature,
a smooth transition from the potential to the actual.
The mighty energy of evil which beats down upon
the world is far too obvious, and causes far too much
anguish, to be escaped; and therefore the dynamism of
the ethical process must be expressible in terms of stress
and struggle; creative equilibrium can only be plausible
if it can be achieved out of the dark underworld of evil
and disintegration, heaven a possibility only as the result
of harrying hell.

If then it is right to think of these things as characteristic of the world of today we can now make a summary
picture of some of its main tendencies as the search for a
way of life which will both enlarge the personality and
discover the way to community; which at the same time
will face the dark facts squarely and turn them into the
material of a life which is purposive because creative, and
which, being creative, may resolve the many-levelled
tensions which distract the soul of man.

Let us now turn to the thomist moral theory, and examine the extent to which it can show itself relevant to these needs.

For St. Thomas, the moral life is simply the *motus in Deum*, the movement of the personality to fullness of life in God. A great deal of harm has been done by simply lifting the second part of the *Summa Theologica* out of its place in the whole work, and treating it as though it thus in isolation gave a complete picture of St. Thomas's view of the moral life. The second part is precisely a part of a whole. It is determined by what precedes and what follows. In isolation therefore it is like a severed human hand. The *Summa* as a whole describes a circular movement, from God and back to God; man shares, and in a special way, in this cosmic process; and it is the whole man who thus shares, it is the whole psycho-physical personality, made in the image of the Creator, having dominion over lesser creatures but being himself a part of a greater *civitas*, a spirit world, and living in and acting through the Mediator Christ, and the *Totus Christus* which is Christ in his Mystical Body the Church.

The most obvious thing then about the thomist moral theory is that it is dynamic, that it describes a process, a growth; it is concerned with the movement from the potential to the actual, though it is not the natural potentialities merely that are involved but what are technically called the obediential—the seeds of a life that is divine implanted directly by God.

The second thing to be noted is that this process is precisely a way to the discovery of the Other. It would indeed be possible to describe the Godward movement in terms of what Bremond called panhedonism: a growth to divine life indeed, but in which the accent, the atmosphere, remain egocentric, the aim remains selfish. But for St. Thomas, though man cannot but desire to be happy, and is right to see the way to God as the way to happiness, this is not at all the final word. The whole of the moral life is subsumed under religion and ensouled by *caritas*—which means that every act of every virtue is meant to be also an act of worship and an act of love—and it is this that gives it its specific orientation. In this ideal there is no danger of loss of selfhood and absorption in God; but equally there is no danger of trying to subordinate the immensities of God to the demands of the ego. There is in man the double urge, to give and to receive: it is love that shows us how to fuse these two contrary forces into one by teaching us that, where there is love, giving is itself a receiving, and that therefore we are most fully ourselves when we most fully and unreservedly give ourselves to the Other: we find our life by losing it. Self-realization ceases to be selfish when it discovers the true nature of love.

Let us return now to the idea of tension. St. Thomas presents us with a creative morality: the self is enlarged, the personality fulfilled, through the moral and intellectual virtues, through art and love and society and, over all, through the habitual grace which is the shared life of God. But in all these creativities there is tension; and between these various creativities there is tension; and how are the tensions to be resolved? There is a little article in the *IIa IIae* which describes how conflicts of duties are to be decided by the fact that some beings have greater claims on our love than others; and the principle can bear a wider application than its immediate context. *In la sua volontade è nostra pace*: his *will* is our peace: if love is really suffusing the personality and directing the dynamism of human activity, then, just as the tension between self-interested and disinterested love is resolved, so also these other tensions can be resolved, eventually and after much toil and many tears, in the complete identity of will, begotten of love, between creature and Creator—that identity of will which is both perfect obedience and perfect freedom—the freedom of the sons of God.

The mention of toil and tears brings us to the idea of ethical unrest and the need of the dark journey. The second part of the *Summa* is set against the background not only of the power and providence of God but also of the fall of man and the power of Satan. St. Thomas would not be surprised at the vagaries of Eros as described by a Denis de Rougemont; he would not be surprised to hear of Satan-worship or Satanic possession; the influence of the powers of darkness in the world is a commonplace to him. Aristotle does not treat of humility, but St. Thomas asks whether it is not the *potissima virtutum*, the most powerful of all virtues, and answers that it is at any rate in one sense the foundation of the spiritual edifice. He is no stranger to the idea that re-birth into the adoption of sons implies a preceding death and burial with Christ; nor to man's need of poverty of spirit if he is to discover a new heaven and a new earth. The metaphysical abyss which separates creature from Creator is widened by the ethical abyss of sin: there is no progress except in and through the redeeming Christ. Grace is not at a tangent to nature, it is the healing and elevating of nature; but it is not magic, it implies for its effectiveness the effort of a humble and contrite heart. Indeed at the very core of St. Thomas's teaching there is the specifically christian tension between what we might call eudaemonism and eschatology: on the one hand, the view of morality as self-fulfilment in the sense in which we have been considering it, a fulfilment which includes the building of the earthly city and the perfecting of the natural powers in God's service; on the other hand, the view of the Godward journey in terms of the transitoriness and unimportance of earthly life, the sense of doom

and judgement and the consequent flight from the world
and the things of the world. In theory as well as in practice,
christians have often evaded the tension by ranging themselves exclusively on the one side or the other; for St.
Thomas, who saw the truth in both sides, that was not
possible. Did he succeed in resolving the tension?

Let us first of all remind ourselves that his eudaemonism
does include the building of the earthly city; and that this
building is a work in which, as M. Maritain has pointed
out so clearly, christian and non-christian can join together, The growth to fullness which the moral theory
describes is primarily a growth to supernatural fullness, the
sharing of the life of God; but we are to achieve that fullness through living the life of this earth, through the
exercise and the fulfilment of our natural powers; and so
the supernatural end includes a natural end; and though
that natural end is, by the very fact of its inclusion in the
greater thing, essentially changed from the eudaemonism
of an Aristotle, it still remains true that it involves purposes which can be and should be acceptable to the non-
christian precisely because they *can* be viewed in terms of
the finite and earthly happiness of man: they do corres-
pond to the root demands of human nature as such.

Let us also recall that this natural pattern of human life
and social progress is expressed for St. Thomas in the
natural law, for the natural law is precisely the statement
of the intrinsic structure of human nature and therefore of
human life; and here again therefore he has much to say
that may gain the interest of those who are looking for a
stable foundation for international society. And this becomes all the clearer when we remember that the natural
law as he thus views it is indeed an eudaemonist concept:
is indeed a question of producing certain consequences
and not an arbitrary ruling regardless of consequences: is

indeed the way to progress and peace and therefore happiness.

But when you have viewed the thomist moral theory from this eudaemonist angle you are then brought up against the apparently contradictory aspect, the eschatological. St. Thomas knows as well as any other christian that the heart must be set against anything that can withdraw it from God; that the fashion of this world passeth away, as St. Paul tells us, who would have those that use the world be as though they used it not. Created things, says St. Thomas himself, are darkness compared with the immensity of the divine light; and he repeats the words of the *Book of Wisdom,* that they are as a stumbling-block to the feet of the foolish, keeping them from their true end which is God.

How can you be as though not using the world and at the same time be concerned with the building of the temporal city? Once again we shall find the answer in *caritas*, man's God-given love of God; which puts man in immediate relationship with God and, inspiring all his actions whether they be concerned with the inner life of spirit or with the affairs of the world, gives them precisely the quality of detachment. To care and not to care: you use all the energy you have in building the temporal city since this is part of the cosmic return to God; but for that very reason too your building is primarily an act of love for him, an act of *caritas*. And the dynamism of *caritas* includes, for St. Thomas, those direct impulsions of the Spirit upon the soul which are called the gifts of the holy Ghost, and especially the gift of wisdom—the wisdom which is neither that of the philosopher nor that of the theologian but which is a sort of intuition divinely given to the heart, enabling it to judge *per altissimas causas,* by ultimates and as though with the eyes of God. And what does that imply?

It implies that, as created things in themselves are revealed anew in the light of his omnipresence, so too the character of human events and ambitions is revealed anew in the light of his love and his will. I must love my cat because it is *his* cat.

Those in whom the Spirit is thus active are indeed *quasi non utentes,* are indeed as having nothing and possessing all things; they have learnt to care and not to care; all things are theirs to enjoy because creatures are not stumbling-blocks for them but stepping-stones, not a distraction from God but a constant reminder of God—why? Because their love of them is become a part of their love of God, their attitude to them determined by their desire of his will; and so they work with them and for them as long as the day lasts, but are ready to give them back into his hands when the night cometh when no man can work. If, for example, you were to take the question of christian marriage, of which St. Paul is speaking in the passage from *I Corinthians,* and were to attempt a statement of its principles, first from the point of view of thomist eudaemonism and then from that of pauline (or thomist) eschatology, you would reach the same conclusion: you would find that, here as elsewhere, fulfilment and detachment go together; you would find that, here as elsewhere, it is only the poor in spirit who are happy, who are the real creators, and who can bring glory to the earth.

The idea of using all one's *energies* has just been mentioned; and it suggests a further point. The world of today is not interested in the sort of bland and suave urbanities which have sometimes been associated with ethical theorizings. It is possible to paint a picture of the Good Life which turns it into a perquisite of the privileged and leisured classes—whoever they, nowadays, may be. *Surtout,* said Talleyrand, *point de zèle.* It is that sort of atmosphere, the cultured distaste for the romantic in thought and in life, with which a world in crisis can have no sympathy. And people sometimes associate the thomist moral theory with something of the sort because of its adoption of the aristotelean doctrine of the golden mean. (The unfortunate ambiguity of the very word mean is not forgotten.) But there is here a sad misunderstanding. The golden mean is thought of as being like the church of Laodicea, neither hot nor cold and therefore worthy of being spewed out of the mouth. But *virtus stat in medio* merely states a psychological fact. Vices go in contrasting pairs: you can be either cruel or soft, either foolhardy or timorous, either a spendthrift or a miser; and rightness consists in avoiding both of these extremes and finding the truth which lies between them: the gentleness which is also strong, the bravery which is also intelligent, the openhandedness which can use means and not be used by them. But all this has nothing to do with the *intensity*, the ardour, with which actions of these kinds are performed. When you have found where gentleness or generosity or bravery lie, then of course the ardour with which you do what is to be done will depend in the last resort on the ardour of the *caritas* which is in you—and there is no question of limitation, of careful correctitude, there. Love can always be strong as death, whether it is expressing itself in bravery or in prudence, in generosity or in planning for the morrow.

And what of the problem with which we began, the search for a synthesis between individualism and totalitarianism? What has thomism to say of community? Here again you reach the same conclusion whether you proceed eudaemonistically or eschatologically, from the notion of the growth of personality or from a purely otherworldly concentration on the figure of Christ as the *caput omnium hominum*, the Head of humanity.

For St. Thomas as for Aristotle man is a social animal; if he is to reach the fullness of his stature it must normally be by living the social life, and society is in that sense one of the factors which build up the total personality. But we are still in the realm of justice and charity: a right implies a corresponding duty; and it is in fact in the carrying out of those duties, in serving society, that man can be helped by society to his fullness. He receives, but he must also give; and here again the giving *is* a receiving. But to give he must be a personality: the error of totalitarianism is to suppose that a human *civitas* can be built by individuals who are subhuman. The nation—and ultimately the world—must be a community of persons as a family is a community of persons: the family is built by the personal contributions of its members, and its members are fulfilled in the common life of the family. Fulfilled, not submerged: giving, but giving as persons. If you were to say to any modern community centre, This will go wrong if it is regimented, you would be talking as a thomist; and no doubt the people concerned would agree with you . . .

But precisely because you give as a person there is an element of reticence, there are reserves: not in any sense a lack of generosity—it is not at all that you give only half your mind to it—but a recognition that the personality does live in greater worlds than this, has weightier allegiances, deeper loves; and so here too it is a question of caring and not caring; which is why we are told that the meek, the humble (because humility is only poverty of spirit applied to immaterial as well as material things) shall possess the earth.

That is why you reach an identical conclusion from whichever end you start. If you think of human society in terms of human fulfilment and happiness, then of course you throw yourself heart and soul into the affairs of the everyday world, loving its beauty, labouring to heal its wounds and to build always better than before. But if you think of human society in terms of the Mystical Body of Christ, and therefore of duty to one's neighbour in terms not of this world but of the next, it still remains that the material of *caritas* is equally the life of this world, the things of this world; and you use them *quasi non utentes* but the fact remains that you do use them, do love them, and that they can be of otherworldly significance only in the degree to which you use them and love them wholeheartedly.

Let us add one final thought. We are living in a world over which there hangs a sword of Damocles; and the apocalyptic sense of doom may lead some to abandon their creative opportunities—as people for instance refuse to have children—in spite of their creative impulses. To do that is to precipitate a mental crisis: if we adopt that policy the decline of the West will become a Gadarene rout. But one might well question whether there is any way whatsoever out of that impasse except the way of christian humanism, of caring and not caring; and for that reason alone therefore, even if there were no other, it seems permissible to affirm that St. Thomas's moral theory has indeed something helpful to suggest to modern man.